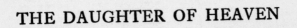

THE DAUGHTER OF HEAVEN

THE DAUGHTER
OF HEAVEN

BY

PIERRE LOTI AND JUDITH GAUTIER

Translated by RUTH HELEN DAVIS

NEW YORK
DUFFIELD & COMPANY
1912

Preface

Thoroughly to understand China, one must realize that it has for three hundred years cherished in its heart a deep and continually bleeding wound. When the country was conquered by the Manchus of Tartary, the ancient dynasty of the Mings was forced to yield the throne to the Tzin invaders, but the Chinese nation never ceased to mourn the ancient dynasty nor to hope for its restoration. Revolution is therefore a permanent thing in China—a fire which smoulders eternally, breaking into flame in one province only to be smothered and blaze out again presently in another.

No doubt the Yellow Empire is too immense to permit of complete understanding among the revolutionaries, or of collective effort to break off the Tartan yoke. Several times, nevertheless, the Chinese race has been near to victory. When, some twenty years ago, certain events, which Europe never really understood, brought about an upheaval in China, the revolutionaries, victorious for a time, proclaimed at Nang-King an emperor of Chinese blood and of the dynasty of the Mings. His name was Ron-Tsin-Tse, which means: The Final Flowering, and by the faithful his era was called Tai-Ping-Tien-Ko, which is as much as to say: The Empire of the Great Celestial Peace. He reigned seventeen years, concurrently with the Tartar Emperor at Pekin and almost within the shadow of that city.

Later, the authorities forced a complete suppression of his history: all records of it were confiscated and burned, and men were forbidden, under penalty of death, even to utter his name. Here, however, is the translation of a passage relating to him which occurs in a voluminous report addressed by the Tartar general Tsen-Konan-Wei, to the Emperor at Pekin:

"When the revolutionaries rose in the province of Chan-Tung (he says) they possessed themselves of sixteen provinces and six hundred cities. Their guilty chief and his criminal friends had become really formidable. All their generals fortified themselves in the places they had taken, and not until they had stood three years of siege were we again Masters in Nang-King. At this time the rebel army numbered more than two hundred thousand men, but not one of them would surrender. The moment they perceived themselves lost they set fire to the palace and burned themselves alive. Many of the women hanged or strangled themselves, or threw themselves into the lakes in the gardens. However, I succeeded in making one young woman prisoner, and pressed her to tell me where the Emperor was. 'He is dead,' she replied; 'vanquished, he poisoned himself.' But immediately the new Emperor was proclaimed in the person of his son, Hon-Fo-Tsen. She led me to the old Emperor's tomb, which I ordered broken open. In it was found in fact the Emperor's body, enveloped in a shroud of yellow silk embroidered with dragons. He was old, bald, and had a white mustache. I caused his body to be burned and his ashes to be thrown to the winds. Our soldiers destroyed all that remained within the walls: there were three days and nights of killing and pillage. However, one troop of several thousands of rebels, very well-armed, succeeded in escaping from the city, dressed in the costumes of our dead, and it is to be feared that the new Emperor was able to escape with them."

This Emperor, Hon-Fo-Tsen, who, in fact, did succeed in fleeing from Nang-King, was looked upon by the real Chinese as their legitimate sovereign, and his descendants in secret no doubt reigned after him uninterruptedly.

Several years ago a very remarkable man, who seemed to incarnate in himself the new China, dreamed of a pacific and genuine reconciliation of the two inimical races. (He had many dreams indeed: one of them, for instance, that of founding the United States of the World.) He conceived the almost unrealizable project of converting to his ideas the Emperor at Pekin himself and of securing his help to reform China without the spilling of any blood. His name was Kan-You-Wey. To get near the Emperor he opened a school at Pekin in 1889.

Many rumors, though very conflicting ones, were in circulation concerning the personality of this invisible Emperor Kwang-Su, kept as he was under strict guardianship, like a captive in the heart of his palace and so unknown to everyone. Some versions declared him alert, well-read, interested in modern things; others represented him as feeble in body and spirit, given to excesses and incapable of action.

Kan-You-Wey would believe only in the favorable version: he knew besides what the ministers of the Dowager Regent were worth, masters with her of the Imperial power. He pitied the Imperial victim. His whole heart turned toward his sovereign because he was unhappy. How could he reach him in his quadrupled walls? How win the attention of his melancholy idol? Kan-You-Wey ten times renewed his attempts, with the zeal of an apostle, and succeeded finally, in 1898, thanks to one of his disciples, in putting before the Emperor a memorial that he had prepared for him.

Then the phantom-sovereign roused himself. Much struck with these insurgent ideas, he wanted them explained to him in detail, and gave an audience to the reformer. He surrendered at once to the influence of this great spirit, made him his minister, intimate and confidant; and, sustained by his counsel, achieved at last the control of his affairs.

It is at this moment of the reign of Kwang-Su that our play takes place. The Emperor himself is the hero, and Kan-You-Wey figures in it under the name of Fount-in-the-Forest.

JUDITH GAUTIER AND PIERRE LOTI.

Act   I—First Tableau.
    The Gardens of the Palace at Nang-King.

    Second Tableau.
    The Throne Room of the Palace at Nang-King.

Act   II—The Pavilion of the Empress.

Act III—Interior of the Imperial Citadel at Nang-King.

Act IV—First Tableau.
    The Place of Execution at the Base of the Ramparts, Pekin.

    Second Tableau
    The Grand Throne Room in the Palace at Pekin.

DRAMATIS PERSONÆ

THE EMPEROR OF PEKING, a Tartar of the Tsing (Pure) Dynasty (aged 30)

FOUNT-IN-THE-FOREST, Councillor to the Tartar Emperor

ARROW-BEARER
FAITHFUL PRINCE } Chinese dignitaries of the Court of Nanking
WINGED PRINCE

THE SON OF SPRINGTIME, the little Chinese Emperor at Nanking (aged seven or eight)

VEILED-LIGHT, the Empress's Councillor

CHIEF ASTROLOGER

A TARTAR GENERAL

POPLAR, a high Mandarin

ROCK
FIR-SAPLING } Gardeners at the Nanking Palace
HUMPBACK
STRONG-ARM

TWO TARTAR SPIES

TWO TARTAR EXECUTIONERS

AN EUNUCH

THE DAUGHTER OF HEAVEN, Chinese Empress of the Ming (Bright) Dynasty (aged twenty-four or twenty-five)

GOLDEN LOTUS
CINNAMON } Ladies-in-waiting to the Empress
TRANQUIL BEAUTY,
PEARL

Governess of the Palace at Nanking
Governess of the Palace at Peking
Street Vendors of Sweetmeats and Flowers at
 Peking
High Mandarins, Common People, Chinese and
 Tartar Soldiers

TIME: China at the Present Day

ACT I

THE GARDEN OF THE PALACE AT NAN-KING.

*To the left, the pavilion of the ladies-in-waiting, in
front of which is a flower-wreathed verandah,
Through the trees and the bushes in full bloom,
roofs of yellow earthenware, with upturned
gable-ends and decorated with monsters, can
be seen. Great twisted cedars, pools, rivulets,
curved bridges of marble and red lacquer.
Preparations are on foot for a fête. In the
background servants are setting up banners,
lances, and emblems of every shape. In the
foreground, gardeners are putting the garden
in order and sweeping away the rain of flowers
which has fallen from the trees. The sun is
rising.*

The Daughter of Heaven

SCENE I

Rock, Fir Sapling, Strong-arm, Humpback, *gardeners. In the distance a bell and a drum can be heard.*

Rock

[*Stopping his work and listening.*] *Do you hear* the great bronze bell and the drum? Another Prince is passing through the Gateway of State and making his entrance into our Palace of Nanking.

Fir-Sapling

Yes, I hear —— but I would rather see.

Strong-arm

Beautiful sights are not for us to see.

Rock

The great ceremonies do not need the gaze of such as us.

Fir-Sapling

Yes! we know that. Our duty is to work on in silence,— patiently to prepare the beauty of the festival which is not for our eyes.

Strong-arm

Are you complaining? —— Every creature must accept the place in life which falls to its lot.

Rock

That law governs all. There are some animals that are proud and splendid, birds with magnificent plumage, and there are also rats and horrible insects, which inspire loathing.

Strong-arm

Among trees there are kings, and among flowers princesses.

Rock

And many poor plants have neither beauty nor perfume.

Fir-Sapling

The rain refreshes them just the same, and the sun warms them.

Humpback

It sometimes happens that chance favours the most humble. Listen to me. Though I was in no way to blame, I have witnessed a sight which I was forbidden to see.

Strong-arm

You? You have witnessed such a sight?

Fir-Sapling

What was it? Tell us.

HUMPBACK

Well, it was yesterday, after sundown. The other gardeners had just gone away; I had not yet finished my task, but remained to polish one of those great marble lions, at the Gateway of State. I was working all unsuspicious, when suddenly I heard the great drum and the clanging of the bell, and I saw the watchers descend from their tower to open the great gate. The guards and generals and ministers were all running. I heard it said that the new arrival was the most important of all the invited guests, the Viceroy of the Southern Provinces. How could I make my escape in the midst of all these wonderful personages? It was impossible! I hid behind one of the huge paws of the lion and made myself very small. No one took any notice of me —— and I saw, I saw through the pierced globe, you know, which the lion holds in his clutch ——.

FIR-SAPLING

You saw the Viceroy of the South enter with his retinue? ——

Yes, I saw! Oh! such costumes of silk and gold! Such horses shining with gems! Such banners! And some terrible faces, too, some glances awful in their pride! —— But when he came, oh! then I understood that besides him all the others counted for naught. He was pale, with a very weary air, on a horse led by two attendants —— His costume was simple, but seemed richer than all the others —— He was so imposing that my heart would no longer beat in my breast, and it seemed to me that if only he turned his unseeing eyes towards me, I should drop dead.

FIR-SAPLING

Ah, was it like that? If one feels like that for no more than a Viceroy, how would it be if one were gazed upon by the Emperor himself?

HUMPBACK

But I assure you, no one who has not seen him can ——

FIR-SAPLING

Hush! Hush! Here comes a Palace official.

SCENE II

ROCK, FIR-SAPLING, STRONG-ARM, HUMPBACK, ARROW-BEARER, a Palace official.

ARROW-BEARER

So this is the way you do your work? You fritter away in foolish chatter the few precious moments which are left.

HUMPBACK

The work will be finished, my Lord.

ARROW-BEARER

Will be finished! What, when I see the ground still strewn with petals and dead flowers —— and here, of all places, around the Pavilion of the Ladies-in-Waiting. [*Aside*] where blooms that living flower whom I adore.

HUMPBACK

No sooner have we put all straight than the spiteful wind shakes the branches and we have to begin all over again.

ARROW-BEARER

Remove them from the moss, at all events —— Those faded flowers look like so many stains.

SCENE III

ROCK, FIR-SAPLING, STRONG-ARM, HUMPBACK, ARROW-BEARER, GOLDEN LOTUS, CINNAMON, PEARL, TRANQUIL BEAUTY — *Ladies in Waiting.*
The ladies appear hestitatingly on the verandah of the Pavilion. GOLDEN LOTUS *advances and rests her elbows on the balustrade.* ARROW-BEARER *gazes upon her with evident emotion.*

CINNAMON [*in a whisper*]

I thought I recognised the voice of my lord Arrow-Bearer.

TRANQUIL BEAUTY

Golden Lotus recognised it before you.

PEARL

That young man is always stealing about here.

TRANQUIL BEAUTY

We all know the reason.

CINNAMON

See, he greets our companion as if she were a Queen.

TRANQUIL BEAUTY

Is she not the Queen of his heart?

ARROW-BEARER

The breeze of spring time caresses me gently and intoxicates me with the perfume of the lotus.

TRANQUIL BEAUTY

The allusion is evident.

CINNAMON

It is well known that The breeze of spring-time signifies love.

PEARL

And her name is Golden Lotus.

GOLDEN LOTUS [*to* ARROW-BEARER]

My lord, I heard that you ordered the flowers to be removed —— Was I misinformed?

ARROW-BEARER

I dared to raise my voice to give that order ——
Can I have displeased you?

GOLDEN LOTUS

Oh! no —— But I desire to ask your indulgence
for the lovely dead flowers. Permit them to remain there as a carpet at the foot of our pavilion.
Though broken from their stems, they are still beautiful and keep their perfume.

ARROW-BEARER

What glory for me to obey you! I envy those
flowers which will be trod by your little feet.

[*He makes a sign for the gardeners to with-
draw.*]

TRANQUIL BEAUTY

[*Pulling at the sleeve of* GOLDEN LOTUS]
Enough, Golden Lotus. It is not proper for us
to listen to such remarks.

ARROW-BEARER

Have you nothing more to say to me?

TRANQUIL BEAUTY

Let us go. Come, we must return to the Pavilion.

GOLDEN LOTUS [*to Tranquil Beauty*]

No, stay a moment.

[*to* ARROW-BEARER]
My lord, you know news travels slowly to the

quarters of the Ladies-in-Waiting, and my curiosity is eager on this most solemn day, when our Empress is to restore the throne of the bright dynasty of the Mings and to take on her the regency of the Empire. At what precise hour will the festival begin? —— Do you know the order of the ceremonies?

Arrow-Bearer

What great pleasure for me to be able to inform you. The Criers of the Minister of Rites proclaimed last night the order of the ceremonies. I have taken note of what I heard.

[*He takes from his sleeve a small scroll.*]

I hope to write several poems about this later. It is a date quite unique in the annals of China.

Golden Lotus

Oh! read it to us, my lord.

[*The young girls eagerly gather about* Arrow-Bearer.]

Arrow-Bearer   [*reading*]

" On this holy day on which our Empress, laying aside her mourning for her illustrious Husband, is about to take up the power in the name of Her son, in defiance of that usurper who for three hundred years has held all China under his yoke: An order to all high Dignitaries of the Palace, to the Masters of the Ceremonies, to the Grand Secretaries of State, to the Ministers, Warriors, and Princes, to the Guardians of the Imperial Seal! Let them hold themselves in readiness before the last watch of night and gather together all the precious objects which they have in their keeping so as to place them, according to the due rites, on the six golden tables in the Palace of Great Purity. Let the Master-in-Chief of the Music place orchestras and singers in the galleries and in the Throne-room. As soon as the last watch shall have sounded, let the Astrologer go to inform Her Majesty the Empress that the chosen hour has come when she must repair to the Temple of her Ancestors to offer the prescribed sacrifices to the August Shades. Her Majesty will be attended only by the Princesses and Her Ladies-in-Waiting.

TRANQUIL BEAUTY

By us! —— Then let us return to the Pavilion, we must prepare at once.

GOLDEN LOTUS

We shall be told when it is time.

ARROW-BEARER [continuing to read]

From the Temple of Ancestors to the Palace of Great Purity, let all Dignitaries, Officers, Guards, Secretaries form up in a line on either side of the road along which the Empress will pass in a palanquin, ornamented with dragons and phoenixes, to the foot of the staircase leading to the throne-room, where the grand ceremony of investiture will take place.

Golden Lotus

Will women be present at that?

Arrow-Bearer

Yes, the Princesses and the Ladies-in-Waiting will form the retinue of the Empress and group themselves about her.

Golden Lotus

Ah! I was not sure —— It was that particularly which I wished to know.

Arrow-Bearer

The young Emperor will be close to the brave mother who is to reign in his name. Reign, you know how! Reign in mystery, in anguish, faced by insurmountable difficulties ——

Golden Lotus

How many hearts beat for Her, how many strong arms are ready to defend Her!

Tranquil Beauty

Have all the invited guests arrived at the Palace?

Arrow-Bearer

I believe so. The most powerful of all, the Viceroy of the South, has been lodged not far from here, in the Pavilion of Limpid Fountains. If the bushes were not so leafy you would be able to see the roof of his residence from your Pavilion.

Cinnamon [*In a whisper*]

I should love to get a look at the Prince.

Golden Lotus

One question more, my Lord. Does not some new danger threaten us? Dark rumours have reached us —— Are our reconquered Provinces well garrisoned?

Arrow-Bearer

Alas! even during the hours of joy, anxiety assails us. Alas that, when the delicious perfume of a flower caresses us, we must watch with dread the storm which is always threatening on the horizon. The gazelle had a little respite because the tiger was wounded. If he recovers, he will immediately begin again the pursuit of his prey.

Golden Lotus

What is the meaning of that allusion?

Arrow-Bearer

That the Tartar Emperor, who reigns at Peking and considers us, the dispossessed Chinese, as rebels, has just been vanquished in the war which the dangerous Western Barbarians made against him. With great difficulty he has obtained peace, and he has not yet recovered from the effects of his defeat.

GOLDEN LOTUS

Ah! yes, the rumor of that war came to us.   But what was the cause of it?

TRANQUIL BEAUTY

How politics interest her!

PEARL

Yes! when that young man is her teacher.

ARROW-BEARER

The cause of it was peculiar.   A Prince, kinsman to the Tartar usurper, conceived the foolish idea of mustering an army of bandits to hurl upon the hated Christians in the north of China.   But the horde, once let loose, got out of hand.   It rushed against the barbarian strangers, whose presence has for a long time been tolerated in the neighbourhood of the Palace.   Then the armies of the Western nations came to sack Peking, whence the Tartar Emperor fled with his entire Court.

GOLDEN LOTUS

Doubtless it is unhappy for us that the usurper has made peace ——

ARROW-BEARER

Who knows?   Perhaps China might have fallen under a more evil dominion still.

TRANQUIL BEAUTY

Is the lesson not finished yet?

GOLDEN LOTUS [*withdrawing*]

It is time, my lord, for us to prepare for the festival.

ARROW-BEARER

It is you who will beautify the setting.

GOLDEN LOTUS

Ah, do not make sport of me —— until we meet again, my lord.

ARROW-BEARER

[*Seeing someone come from the right.*]

Go into the house quickly! Your illustrious neighbour, the Viceroy of the South, is walking in the garden and comes this way.

TRANQUIL BEAUTY

[*Lowering a bamboo blind*]

If we could only see him through the blind! ——

ARROW-BEARER

Farewell! I must give place to a nobler visitor.

[*The young girls go in, and* ARROW-BEARER *hurries off.*]

SCENE IV

The TARTAR EMPEROR, *disguised as the Viceroy of the South, with* FOUNT-IN-THE-FOREST, *his minister.*

FOUNT

I see no one —— Your Majesty may come forward.

EMPEROR

Your Majesty!   Do you wish to ruin me?

FOUNT

Oh! Sire.

EMPEROR

Again!

FOUNT

When we are alone, I cannot refrain ——

EMPEROR

You must —— Behind those blinds, probably spies are watching us.

FOUNT

Eaves-droppers, rather.   That is the Pavilion of Ladies-in-Waiting.

EMPEROR

The Pavilion of the Ladies-in-Waiting —— So there are also Ladies-in-Waiting here?   In very truth, it seems to me that I am dreaming.   Yet I knew what I came hither to find that after three centuries of reign the Emperors of my dynasty had never succeeded in subduing the secret resistance of the conquered — I knew that.   That in the Southern Provinces the rebels had never yet bowed the head,

aye, I knew that.   That Nanking was their capital
and that here a descendant of the Mings had even
reigned.   For more than seventeen years before being crushed by our armies, of all that I was aware
—— But I thought this phantom empire was more
mysterious, more hidden in the dark, and here I find
a palace as beautiful as mine, with guards, dignitaries, ministers, a ceremonial regulated as at my
own Court —— Our Empire is too large it seems,
to be governed by one head alone —— I wished to
see with my own eyes.   I was prepared for all sur-
prises, yet this is beyond me.

[*He sits down on a bench under a tree in full
bloom.*]

FOUNT

What is more surprising still is that you are here
unknown to all; here in the midst of your implacable
enemies, and clad in the fashion of three hundred
years ago.

EMPEROR

It is a happy coincidence that this Viceroy of the
South whose place I have taken is of my build ——
What can he be thinking of this adventure, in the
ship where he is now held a prisoner for me?   What
can he imagine, do you suppose?

FOUNT

Anything — except the truth.

EMPEROR

Yet if he should escape, would I not be lost indeed?

FOUNT

My heart feels as though in a vice. Are you not lost in any case?

EMPEROR

Silence! After all, what have I to risk? My life? Under the shadow of that throne from which they would banish me, is not life an unending agony? With what crushing weight do the slow hours fall upon me. Who can describe the horror of that indolent stagnation, of that idle solitude? Oh! the rage which consumes the soul, when one is the Master and yet has no power! If I find death here, I shall be a thousand times happier for having come. All my unhappy existence down to the present has not been worth as much to me as these last few days of flight and travel, this rapture of escape, for a time, from that grey, silky web wherein I am a prisoner. Oh! to work, to work in the sunshine, to work like a man, to attempt some daring act, which, if I die, will at least remain behind to honour my memory.

FOUNT

You are wonderful, you are noble, you are fearless. But I, who am as nothing, I have the right to tremble.

EMPEROR

It is you, however, who have awakened my spirit, who have aroused it from its deadly torpor; it is you who have inspired me with will and strength. Have you not approved of my project? Have you not found noble, and worthy of a sage, the dream which carried me away.

FOUNT [*kneeling before the* EMPEROR]

I cried aloud with enthusiasm, I wept with emotion when I grasped your sublime thought —— But it is an impossible dream, and the wish to realise it is a madness as generous as it is vain. I fear for you, Sire, my well beloved Master, I fear!

EMPEROR

You fear what? Up to to-day has not my plan worked out as if by magic.

FOUNT

Up to to-day, yes, I cannot deny it.

EMPEROR

My departure from the Palace, which seemed so perilous — not an obstacle! You, my dear minister, enter your official palanquin, I was at your side in the costume of your Secretary! I smiled, you remember, like a schoolboy playing truant. My manner was so gay as to frighten you.—— And your poor little secretary, your pupil, as dear to you as a son, consented to take my place in my bed with its funereal silk draperies, in that sepulchral chamber, railed and walled in again and again, where one stifles with the perfumes which are too sweet. If I come through safe, what can I do in recognition of this boy's tremendous devotion, who acted as substitute for the martyr which I was, who entered into the mummied body of an Emperor of China?

FOUNT

Will he know how to play the part which he assumed?

EMPEROR

Oh! it is an easy part, that of sovereign in my sad, closed room. One sleeps, reads, meditates, and keeps one's self from doing more. I have made use of the weapon which is so often used against me. I have been accused of being ill when I am not so. This time it is I that pretend. Who will dare to doubt?

FOUNT

And the doctor who is taking care of the mock Emperor — are you sure of his fidelity?

EMPEROR

My doctor? What interest would he have in betraying me? He thinks I am engaged in some affair of gallantry and I have promised him a province if my absence is not discovered. He is watching

his patient carefully and has strictly forbidden anyone to go near him.

FOUNT

That is capital!

EMPEROR

Even in my city of Peking there is no risk of my
being recognised, since none of my subjects have
even seen my face.   Flight is made easy for an invisible emperor!   And once on the ship — so
freighted with your anxiety, do you remember?
what rapture it was to fly through space, light as the
cloudlets of smoke which followed in our track!

FOUNT

It is true, the kidnapping of the Viceroy and his
companions was the more dangerous feat, but our
sailors managed it marvellously.   The immortals
are with us, your Majesty.

EMPEROR

Poor little Viceroy!   As the escort who came
to greet him had never seen him, nothing was
simpler than that I should be taken for him.   I told
you, Fount-in-the-Forest, that all must be as simple
as child's-play!

FOUNT

Sire!   Did you compose novels of adventure they
would be more interesting even than those of the
famous Lo Kwan-chung.

EMPEROR

Well, you see, they left me but two things in my splendid solitude; love and opium. Opium exalts the imagination, and I have had plenty of leisure to dream about my plans.

FOUNT

I plan out the future in my writings — prophetically, perhaps, but then I leave to the generations that are to come the duty of fulfilling my prophesies. You, Sire, are offering your own blood as a sacrifice to assuage unconquerable hate. The Immortal gods shall bow to you as to their equal: but those on whom you wish to heap your kindness will destroy you.

EMPEROR

Who knows? Hatred often yields to love.

FOUNT

Not such immemorial hatred as this. Nothing has softened it, and for these three hundred years it has not even known the weakness of a love affair. Never has a Tartar married a Chinese woman, never has a Chinese loved a Tartar woman. During the three years since you issued the decree authorising marriages between the two races, none have availed themselves of the permission.

EMPEROR

Yes, there has been one marriage ———

FOUNT

One marriage! One of your courtiers, to please
you, married the daughter of one of your ministers;
and do you recall the number of favours by which
you have had to repay that act of sacrifice?

EMPEROR

You are, however, a Chinese, and I believe that
you love me a little.

FOUNT

On me alone you have shed the light of your soul;
and I, moreover, have cast away the prejudices
which fetter life. I love you and I admire you.

EMPEROR

Well, that is my recompense ——

FOUNT

Someone is coming! We must take care ——

SCENE V

*Light Palanquins, each carried by two men, stop
before the Pavilion. Two attendants accompany
them and mount the steps.*

FOUNT

Some eunuchs, come, no doubt, to fetch the
Ladies-in-Waiting.

EMPEROR

I thought it was forbidden to employ eunuchs outside of my Palace of Peking!

FOUNT

All privileges are allowed in the Palace of Nanking.

[*They step aside until the Ladies-in-Waiting shall have passed.*]

SCENE VI

The EMPEROR, FOUNT-IN-THE-FOREST, *the* LAIES-IN-WAITING, *and the* EUNUCHS.

TRANQUIL BEAUTY [*In a whisper to* GOLDEN LOTUS]

Those lords are still there.

GOLDEN LOTUS

They have a noble mien.

PEARL

They are secretly watching us.

CINNAMON

Let us pretend that we do not see them.

EUNUCH

The Empress is about to leave Her Palace.   You must continue your gossip to-morrow.

TRANQUIL BEAUTY

If we are late, the fault is yours.

PEARL

You should have informed us sooner.

EUNUCH

Quick, quick, the last watch of night is about to sound.

[*They enter their palanquins, and go on their way in a single file preceded and followed by an* EUNUCH.]

SCENE VII

The EMPEROR *and* FOUNT-IN-THE-FOREST

FOUNT

They are pretty.

EMPEROR

And so gracefully dressed!   It makes me regret the fact that my victorious ancestors imposed the Tartar costume on the people.   These Chinese robes are so much more beautiful.

FOUNT

They make the women appear more slender and delicate.

EMPEROR

Do all the inhabitants of the city garb themselves in the old way?

FOUNT

In their homes, no doubt, they do.   Out of doors, in the streets, they still keep up a pretence of wearing the new.

EMPEROR

The Viceroy whom I sent to Nanking is certainly not ignorant of all this.   Why has he not informed us?

FOUNT

Your Viceroy, Sire, is not a Tartar, but a Chinese, which means that he espouses the cause of the rebels. Yet at Peking, outside the walls of your Palace of Eternal Silence, what goes on is fairly well known. While you are dreaming of ultimate peace, they are preparing for war.

EMPEROR

Alas! ——

[*Trumpets, xylophones and gongs are heard in turn, each five times.   Then the watchmen pass slowly.*]

FOUNT

The fifth watch.

EMPEROR

Must we go in?

FOUNT

Not yet. The Empress is going to the Temple of her Ancestors. That will give us a little time.

EMPEROR

The Empress!—— In a few moments I shall see Her! The beautiful vision I have dreamed of is to be destroyed by the actuality —— Ah! this woman, who must have the uttermost horror for me, can have no idea that for months past she has filled all my thoughts, has haunted my solitary hours. If She only knew that the phantom Emperor, isolated in his palace at Peking, wrote poems in her honour night after night!——

FOUNT

She is said to be beautiful and charming, but that is perhaps only a courtier's tale.

EMPEROR

If She is not, then my sacrifice will be only the more meritorious.

FOUNT

Ah! see, there she comes. She is crossing the garden, and, as no one is here, her palanquin is wide open.

Emperor

Ah!

[*Through the flowering bushes he gazes ardently at her. The sound of a march is heard.*]

But I recognise Her, my friend, that woman so beautiful and tender, so noble and delicate, that rare, that imperial flower! —— Friend, what do you think of this omen? It is She, absolutely She — She whom I have seen reflected in the mirror of my dreams ——

Fount

The eyes of the dragon traverse all space.

[*The* Emperor *seats himself again on the bench, leaning on* Fount-in-the-Forest, *almost fainting.*]

Emperor

See how this emotion shatters my strength!

Fount

You are like the sacred lyre, whose strings vibrate at the slightest inspiration.

SCENE VIII

The Emperor *and* Fount-in-the-Forest, *the little* Emperor *of Nanking,—a child of seven or eight years, who enters playing with a shuttle-cock*

in the Chinese fashion, with graceful movements.
Some Royal nurses follow him, two serving-men
remain at the back.

FIRST NURSE [*trying to take the shuttlecock*
away]

Sire, take care not to overheat yourself.

CHILD

No! no! give it back to me; I want to play some
more.

SECOND NURSE [*Respectfully approaching the*
TARTAR EMPEROR]

Sir, no one is permitted to remain in the presence
of our Majesty, the young Emperor.

EMPEROR

It is he!
[*The shuttlecock with which the little* EMPEROR *of*
Nanking is playing falls on the knees of the big
EMPEROR, *who takes it in his hands.*]

CHILD [*To the* SECOND NURSE]

Leave him there, I want him to stay. You see
that he is ill."
[*To the* EMPEROR]
Why are you so pale?   Are you ill?

EMPEROR

No, Sire!   It is emotion which has made me pale.

CHILD

What about?

EMPEROR

At seeing you, perhaps.

CHILD

That is queer.   Do you think I play shuttlecock so well?

EMPEROR

With infinite grace.

CHILD

Soon, during the ceremony, I shall have to be perfectly quiet.   So I am running about now, to have more patience later —— Do you understand?

EMPEROR

[*Handing the child the shuttlecock*]
Do you wish to go on with your game?

CHILD

No! keep it as a gift from me to your son.

EMPEROR

I have no son.

CHILD

Oh, how sad that is! Very well then, keep it just the same, in memory of a child who has no father.

EMPEROR

[*Detaching a jewel from his girdle*]

Thank you! Take this in exchange as a remembrance from a man whose greatest desire is to have you for his son.

CHILD

Oh! thank you ——

FIRST NURSE

Sire, it is time ——

CHILD

It is a little dragon — an Imperial Dragon! I recognise it! But how do you come to have it? You have not the right to wear it! Do not be afraid, I will tell nobody. Good-bye till next time.

EMPEROR

Till next time!

[*The child runs away, followed by his nurses. The* EMPEROR *gazes after him until he is out of sight.*]

SCENE IX

The EMPEROR *and* FOUNT-IN-THE-FOREST

FOUNT

You are still all of a tremble.

Emperor

My trouble is mixed with sweetness —— Would it not seem that Heaven approves of me and will be my ally? This child comes to me, defends me, is uneasy because of my pallor, and gives me his plaything —— Ah! how precious to me is this little gift.

Fount

Yes! I felt with you the emotion of that chance encounter —— But let calm descend upon your soul. You will need all your composure not to betray yourself during the ceremony of the robing, for this time you are not playing the leading part. Do not forget the three obeisances, the nine complete prostrations. You cannot accustom yourself to bend the knee to another.

Emperor

But I know all these fine points of etiquette better than anyone, for am I not condemned always to see men prostrated at my feet, touching the ground with their foreheads?

[Officers, Guards *and* Heralds *enter at the back of the stage and begin to form into lines. Some unfurling banners. The* Chiefs *give out orders*].

Fount

Let us return! It is time, since you must rehearse your speech. Above all, Sire, change nothing in it. I so much fear that you will betray yourself by some imprudent words.

Emperor

It seems too commonplace, that speech of mine —— Since I have seen her, Her, I must compose another ——

Fount

Oh! no, I beg you. You might distract yourself, break off short, or, more likely, let yourself be carried away beyond measure.

Emperor

You may prepare an opium-pipe for me. Then my mind will work with more ease and clearness.

Fount

Oh! you promised me to give up that poison. You know full well that it is the complete destruction of your energies and your will. The exaltation which results from — it, you know very well with what depression you must pay for that later on."

Emperor

Come! come! only one puff. I swear to you this shall be the last.

[*They leave. Trumpet-calls are heard and shouts of command as the curtain falls.*]

SECOND TABLEAU

The throne-room in the palace of Nanking, seen from the side. The EMPRESS *and the throne upon which she is seated appear in profile. The* LITTLE EMPEROR *is seated near her. The throne is raised on a number of steps; the* LADIES-IN-WAITING *are behind the* EMPRESS, *fanning her with large, feathered fans. The bodyguard is placed on the steps of the throne, and each man is holding a censer containing Tibetan incense. All the dignitaries and officials are standing, in order of rank. At the back, across a colonnade, open-air galleries may be seen, in which are musicians and singers. The palanquin of the* EMPRESS, *with its dragons of gold, is also visible. Outside the crowd can be vaguely seen and heard. Opposite the throne, on a platform, are some dancers costumed as armed warriors, standing motionless. Everyone is standing, with the sole exception of the* EMPRESS *and her little son.*

SCENE I

The crowd, the TARTAR EMPEROR *and* FOUNT-IN-THE-FOREST *(the two latter still disguised, but in full official costume), the* FAITHFUL PRINCE.

34

THE CROWD [*crying rhythmically*]

Ten thousand years!

Ten thousand years!

A happy life to our King! A happy and a long life to our King.

Ten thousand years! Ten thousand years.

[*The music continues at the back.*]

TARTAR EMPEROR [*In a whisper to* FOUNT-IN-THE FOREST]

This old palace is infinitely more beautiful than mine. Its art is purer and more exquisite.

FOUNT [*Also in a whisper*]

Our Chinese art, Sire, in all its ancient purity.

EMPEROR [*Smiling*]

You have remained our masters in all things. In comparison with you we shall always be barbarians, we the invaders and the conquerors. Oh! may it be the unique glory of my reign to restore the noble Chinese tradition by fusing the two peoples for all time to come.

FOUNT

Let us not speak so much, well beloved master. We are being watched! And do not forget that soon you must prostrate yourself! ——

EMPEROR

Before Her! Oh! that will be an easy task.

FOUNT

And your speech, I pray, let it be altogether correct and commonplace —— The fascination which She seems to exercise over you terrifies me already.

[*Chorus, singing at the back*]

Forefathers of my race, from Heaven look down
 Upon this palace with benignant eye!
Your son, the chosen of the immortal gods,
 See now I mount the glorious throne on high.

[*The dancers execute three evolutions of the ritual dance known as the Dance of the Feather and of the Flute*]

CHORUS   [*At the back*]

Let but your spirit and your bravery,
 Your virtues be the guidance of my life;
Then shall I triumph over evil foes
 And fear no fortune in the fiercest strife.

[*The dancers execute three more figures.*]

CHORUS   [*Again*]

The Dragon, on my standard there unfurled,
 Bathes his gold scales in Heaven's azure pure.
My reign shall famous be all times to come
 'Neath his protection, powerful and sure.

[*The dancers complete the three last figures*]

MUSIC

[*The master of ceremonies approaches the guardian of the seals salutes him, and with a gesture in-*]

dicates that he is to follow him. He conducts him to a golden table at the back of the stage. The guardian of the Seals, after having bent the knee, takes from that table the great seal of the Empire, which lies on a large salver. The master of the ceremonies then conducts him to the foot of the throne and withdraws. The guardian of the seals bends the knee and offers the seal to the FAITHFUL PRINCE. *When the* FAITHFUL PRINCE *has taken it, the guardian kneels before the throne, makes three prostrations, rises, and withdraws backwards. The* FAITHFUL PRINCE *bends the knee, and holding the salver with both hands, offers it to the* EMPRESS, *then he rises.*]

[The music stops]

FAITHFUL PRINCE *[To the* EMPRESS]

In the name of all the princes here assembled, in the name of the faithful people and of the army ready to die for the Bright Dynasty, I present to Your Majesty the most sacred treasure, the priceless trust which your ancestors have transmitted to us from generation to generation — the Great Seal of State. In giving You this, we recognise you as the Sovereign of the Empire during the minority of your beloved Son. Accept the decree of Heaven with composure and reverence.

[Two LADIES-IN-WAITING *descend the steps of the*

Throne, take the salver and place it on a table
very near the EMPRESS.]

FAITHFUL PRINCE

Oh! Daughter of Heaven, whom we swear to
serve faithfully! To the end that you may accomplish the work of your deified ancestors, never forget the ten precepts which are the rule of conduct of
all sovereigns. As they are engraved here on the
precious jade, it is my privilege to read them to you
this day in the hearing of all.

[*Reading from a block of jade, which is handed to*
him.]

Fear Heaven.

Love the people.

Exalt the soul.

Cultivate the sciences.

Honour merit.

Listen to wise counsels.

Lessen taxes.

Mitigate the laws.

Spare the treasury.

Avoid the allurements of the senses!

Obeying these commands, one is sure to follow in
the right path. But one must advance along this
road without turnings aside or falterings. Oh! our
Sovereign, be attentive and anxious, as though each
hour of the day you carried a chalice filled to the
brim with water not one drop must be spilled. Act

thus, and then your conduct will be just and your dynasty endure eternally ——

ALL

Ten thousand years!
Ten thousand years!

[*The orchestra plays,* FAITHFUL PRINCE *bends the knee, prostrates himself three times, stands, and retires to his place. The music ceases, complete silence reigns, the* EMPRESS *rises.*]

SCENE II

THE EMPRESS, THE CROWD

EMPRESS

Enlighten me, Oh, Divine Reason! Spirits of my ancestors, enter into my spirit, strengthen my weakness, embolden my heart! —— Will these womanly hands have the power to carry on high this sceptre, which is still too heavy for the frail hands of my little son? At least they shall not tremble! They shall hold it with an unrelaxing grasp, which death alone will have the power to unlock. And you will aid me, all of you, my faithful ones, you will aid me with your advice, with your wisdom and your courage.

The name allotted by the Book of Centuries to the last descendant of the Bright Dynasty is: Perfect Harmony Realised. But alas! it seems a faraway dream, this harmony announced in the ancient days of our history, and longed for with many a prayer by our bruised hearts. Instead of this dream of the future, we have the terrible present with its uncertainty, instability, and war! And that Empire, of which you have proclaimed me sovereign, we must reconquer day by day, tearing it fragment by fragment from the grasp of the ravisher.

Ah, how much bloodshed have we seen in the past three centuries! It is a stream purple with blood, on which floats the vessel freighted with our noble hopes! It tosses about, it battles with the tempest, this vessel with the reddened timbers, but it cannot suffer shipwreck, for it stands for justice and right. Some day it shall drop anchor in a peaceful port, the Bright Dynasty shall be re-established for ever — and all our beloved dead, whose bodies are scattered throughout the length and breadth of the land, whose spirits abide in the clouds above, all our unnumbered dead shall then have their magnificent revenge and receive the reward of their martyrdom.

Like everyone of you here assembled, I dedicate my life to that sacred cause; but it suffices not to die without regret, we must fight to the last, we must defend ourselves with our final breath, that our death may be fruitful. To reconquer our country, to break the yoke which dishonours it, let us

make our hearts fearless, our souls implacable.   No
pity nor mercy for the Tartar!   May our heroic
wrath never lessen, nor our holy hate be appeased.

Toward all other living men we know our duties:
good will, compassion, charity.   Whoever these
men may be, whether they come from the north or
the south, or from the covetous west, to all who
shall call themselves our friends, let us extend a
brotherly hand in accordance with that immemorial
tradition, which only our invaders have violated.

I swear to you, oh, shades of my ancestors, and to
you, all my well beloved subjects, I swear to keep
severe watch upon myself, to take good care that I
am not remiss in any of my duties, I swear to be attentive and anxious, as though I carried in my hands
a chalice filled to the brim with water, of which
not one drop must be spilled.   I swear to hold my
head high against the threats of the future, to submit with resignation to cruel fate, and not even to
move an eye-lash if the sword be lifted against me.

[*She resumes her seat upon the Throne.*]

ALL

Ten thousand years!
Ten thousand years!
[*The music recommences at the back.   At a sign
from the Master of Ceremonies, the Mandarins
leave their places and arrange themselves in several
lines at the foot of the Throne.*]

Two Heralds

Bend the knee.

[*Other* Heralds *at the doors repeat the order to the crowd on the terrace and in the Court yards.*]

Bend the knee.

[*All the mandarins bend the knee at the same time*]

The Heralds

Prostrate yourselves.

Heralds at the Doors

Prostrate yourselves.

[*All the mandarins prostrate themselves three times, touching the ground with their foreheads three times at each prostration.*]

The Heralds

Arise.

Heralds [*At the doors*]

Arise.

[*All the mandarins rise and resume their places.*]

A Herald

Let the Viceroy of the South, in the name of all, make reply to Her Majesty.

[*The Master of Ceremonies approaches the* Tartar Emperor *and leads him towards the Throne. The little* Emperor *of Nanking exchanges glances of recognition with the* Tartar Emperor. *He shows him a Golden Dragon, which is hanging on*

a chain round his neck, while the TARTAR EMPEROR
shows him the shuttlecock hidden under his robe.
The EMPRESS, *surprised, questions her son with a*
look.   The child smiles mysteriously and moves
closer to her.   The TARTAR EMPEROR *contemplates*
the EMPRESS *for a few moments, then slowly pros-*
trates himself.   He rises, and the music ceases.]

EMPEROR

Oh, Divine Majesty! I, your slave, and at this
moment one of the first dignitaries of your Court,
why am I so insignificant a thing?   Why is my will
barren, when it is so eager to make a path both
smooth and glorious for your feet?   Oh! at my
powerlessness to crush the menace of fate, what a
tumult of desire and righteous rage disturbs my soul!
And yet the celestial radiance of Your presence il-
lumines and inspires me.   The dazzling light which
emanates from Your Majesty's presence seems to
colour the clouds on the far horizon, to pierce the
shadows, and I see You there, in the great city of
the Tsings.   I see you seated and all powerful, on
the very Throne of the Tartar Emperor; the immense empire, undivided and at peace, extending
under your feet like a carpet of honour.

No! destiny cannot be cruel to you; before Your
sacred presence, its weapons will be dashed to pieces.
Do not the laws of Heaven and earth seem always
to yield to certain superior beings?   Do you re-

member the beautiful favourite, who formerly capti-
vated one of your sovereign ancestors? When the
day arrived on which, having forfeited the Imperial
favour, she was given into the keeping of the executioners, she gazed upon them calmly, and as they
brandished their swords against her, she smiled
sweetly — her only defence. Then they threw their
weapons at her feet, for no one had the courage to
extinguish that radiant smile ——

[*A murmur of astonishment makes itself felt
throughout the crowd.*]

And so you will disarm destiny, and your most
deadly enemies will bend the knee before you ——

[*So saying, he bends his knee*]

THE EMPRESS   [*After a moment of astounded silence, without rising from the Throne*]

Thank you, my noble subject! Your bold words
have surprised us, but have also charmed us. Moreover, the tragic circumstances of our investiture
make excuse for passionate thoughts and excep-
tional speech. Your prophetic vision has touched
us very deeply —— Thanks to you! Thanks to
all!

[*The* TARTAR EMPEROR *rises and resumes his
place. Music March. The* EMPRESS *descends
slowly from her throne; her retinue forms up to
follow her and crosses the stage. She reaches the
terrace where She enters her palanquin decked with
gold dragons. The whole assemblage, without*

leaving their places, bend the knee and then prostrate themselves.]

CHORUS   [*At back of stage*]
Let all happiness and peace
Rule here now and never cease!
Heaven, grant our humble prayer,
Give us blessings mild and fair,
Gentle rain and balmy air!'
Let our pious voices rise
To the gods above the skies!

ALL   [*Interrupting the Choruses*]
Ten thousand years!
Ten thousand years!
[*The great drum and bell are sounded alternately.*]

CURTAIN

ACT TWO

[*The stage setting is all of white marble, glistening in the moonlight. At the centre back is seen the* EMPRESS'S *Pavilion rising upon several terraces of white marble. Its curved roofs are ornamented with monsters and small bells. Leading to the terraces, in the middle of the stage, is an " imperial stair," an inclined plane of white marble, on which an immense dragon is carved in bas-relief; and also, on either side of this, two identical marble staircases bordered by bronze and jade animals and huge censers on marble brackets. Numerous symmetrical kiosks flank the pavilion on this side and that with curved roofs similar to those of the pavilion, ornamented with small bells and monsters.*

As the Curtain rises, no one is on the stage. A gentle breeze causes the small bells to tinkle at the angles of the roofs.]

SCENE I

THE EMPRESS *and* FOUR ATTENDANTS.

[THE EMPRESS *comes out of the pavilion and advances slowly to the edge of the terrace, her eyes raised to the moon.* FOUR ATTENDANTS *follow her, but remain in the background.*]

EMPRESS

[*Halting at the top of the Imperial stair*] *Oh,* Night of enchantment! Pure light and silence cool!—— Oh, scintillating stars, envelope me in your rays! And thou, pale moon, shroud me in thy blue light; calm my soul, cool my fever! [*She commences her descent down the " Imperial Stair," two of her attendants following, one by the staircase on the right, the other by the staircase on the left, regulating their steps according to those of the* EMPRESS *in the middle.*] That dream, that strange dream which has aroused me from my sleep, I still feel the terror of it—— [*Lowering her voice*] The terror and the charm. [*To her attendants*] Let the astrologer be called at once, that he may discover the meaning of this dream and explain it without dissembling. Listen carefully to my words. I was about to become the prey of a serpent with shining scales,— already he was twining

49

about me and slowly choking me with his chilly coils. Fascinated by his steady gaze, I had not the force to struggle; enervated, inert, I surrendered myself, with no repugnance against death. With fear and suffering a languor that was almost a delight was mingled —— A supreme effort of the will, however, extricated me from his grasp, and suddenly aroused from sleep and dreams I found myself regretting those deadly coils which had imprisoned me —— What can this dream portend? [*To the women*] Report what I have told you to the astrologer. Let him question the Unknown, and give me his response here without delay. Go at once! [*Two of the* ATTENDANTS *depart at this command. The* EMPRESS *continues to descend slowly. She is alone in the middle of the Imperial stair, which is very long, and whose white surface seems sown with tiny glistering spangles.*] How the dew sparkles on the marble footpath! It seems like a carpet of stars. But as I walk I put out their light, and my trailing gown changes the little glistening drops into a pool of water, which soaks the hem of my robe. [*She continues to descend.*] Why is there ever before my eyes the image of that man whom I saw this morning for the first time? Why, on this day, when so many heavy duties have devolved upon my weakness, can I recall only that deep and ardent gaze, which met mine with such sovereign audacity? Why was I no more offended

by that gaze than by the rays of the kindly sun
that beat upon my palace? He found me beautiful,
and his admiration for me shone like an ornament
more precious than the Imperial Phœnix of my
head-dress. How well I understood, when he prostrated himself before me, with what feelings he
threw himself at my feet —— And my son ex-
changed glances of recognition with him! How
came he to know him? Why did I not even dare
to ask him, as though to speak of that
man to my own child were criminal? Oh,
kindly powers of the night, spirits of my deified ancestors who are about me in the air, august shades
to whom I have rendered homage in your golden
temples, come to my aid, gather about your unworthy and feeble daughter! That man, that
stranger in my path, on such a day! Oh,
divinities from whom I am descended, take from
my soul the very remembrance of him. In a solemn
vow I have renounced my earthly personality.
Nothing of myself belongs to me. Daughter of
Heaven, Empress and Regent, I am claimed entirely
by my more than human mission —— Help me to
triumph over the weaknesses which were the charm
of life. Aid me to forget that there are flowers and
pearls and perfumes, grant that I may lose con-
sciousness of the fact that love is the only realm of
woman, and beauty her true power. May my breast
from henceforth be only the marble prison of my

frozen heart! Should it revolt and wish to beat again, may my will become its stern gaoler! Aid me, oh, come down, pure spirits of the air! Make me as unyielding as the goddesses of jade, who keep their eyes lowered that they may not see the things of this world!

[*The two attendants return and prostrate them-selves.*]

FIRST ATTENDANT

The astrologer is ready to give your Majesty his answer.

EMPRESS

Let him come!

[*The attendants leave.*]

That serpent which entwined me, Ah! that cannot be he. His commanding gaze, riveted to mine, was noble and open. Why should he appear to me in that hostile and terrible form? No, no! in a soul that has eyes like that treachery cannot flour-ish —— It cannot be he —— and yet I was carried away by that icy embrace. Who else then, in the world could it be?

SCENE II

The same, THE ASTROLOGER

[*He is one hundred years old. He has a white*

beard, stiff and rough.   He is blind, and is led by a
young boy.   He tries to prostrate himself, but the
EMPRESS *stops him.*]

EMPRESS

Remain standing, noble old man.   Your age and
your sightless eyes excuse you from formalities.

ASTROLOGER

My sightless eyes see into the invisible.   My
spirit, meditating through so many days of darkness, is clairvoyant and prophetic.

EMPRESS

How do you explain the mystery of that dream
which obsesses me?

ASTROLOGER

In the guise of a serpent, the dragon has come
to the phœnix to carry her off and to heap on her
his treasures.   But the phœnix has not understood.
He flapped his wings and made his escape.   Let
her take shelter at present from the terrible storm
which, all unwillingly, the dragon brings in his
train.

EMPRESS

These words are more unfathomable than the
dream.

ASTROLOGER

Yet thus the magic numbers have replied.

EMPRESS

Can you not illumine the darkness?

ASTROLOGER

The veil which covers the future may not be torn away.   To raise one corner at the utmost is all that is allowed to us.

EMPRESS

And by that means should one not at least see a faint glimmer?

ASTROLOGER

Take shelter from the terrible storm!   Let the precious torch which shall illumine the future be placed far beyond the reach of the wind.   That is the decree.   There is nothing more.

EMPRESS

It is well.   I will meditate upon these enigmas. Go in peace, noble old man.

ASTROLOGER

May propitious Heaven shower all its blessings on the Bright Dynasty!

[*He retires.   Day breaks, and flower-beds in the foreground, near the incline, come to view.   They are flowers of Imperial yellow.*]

EMPRESS

[*To her attendants*]

For mercy's sake, for once in my life, leave me alone. I need no further attention. Go!

[*The attendants leave and re-enter the Pavilion.*]

SCENE III

THE EMPRESS [*alone*]

The EMPRESS [*at the foot of the imperial stair, leaning on the marble banisters.*] The storm, said the old man —— The storm, it will come from the north as always! —— Black clouds on the horizon, the armies which are marching against my phantom empire. Black clouds, the armies of the Tartar Emperor —— But this torch which shall illumine the future, what it is? Ah! My son, it must be —— Ah, yes, that it is; my son! —— To shelter him, he said, to hide him, to send him far away, perhaps, from this palace that is threatened on all sides; to separate myself from him in this grave danger — that is what is now demanded of me! —— Still more agony and sacrifice! And it is I who am expected to guide a whole people, when I lack the force to guide myself —— Oh you women who can lean on a strong supporting arm, who can depend for help upon the advice of a manly and farseeing mind! Oh you wives who find in the heart of your husbands a refuge in your weak-

ness! But I am the Empress, and the widowed
Empress, all alone and so high that I have no equal
to whom I may confide my anxieties and my weaknesses —— [*She advances to the middle of the
flower-plot*] Come, listen to the confession which
is overpowering me, oh you flowers of early morning, moist with fresh dew! Oh airy spirits which
hover over flower-beds at the dawn of springtime,
hear me, since I must speak and someone must
listen. That man you know, who came yesterday,
whose gaze tyrannical and yet caressing is like none
other's, he has troubled the sad Empress's heart,
and now in the hour of great peril she is no longer
mistress of herself —— He is only one of her
subjects, and yet she would love to obey him ——

SCENE IV

The same, THE GRAND MISTRESS OF THE CERE-
MONIES, TWO ATTENDANTS.

THE GRAND MISTRESS

[*Prostrating herself*] I have to inform your
Majesty that it is almost the hour of morn, fixed
for the farewell audiences.

EMPRESS

It is well. I come.

THE GRAND MISTRESS

All is in readiness for the toilette of the Empress.
What are her orders?

EMPRESS

I shall give audience here, and let the wearisome
ceremony be made as simple as may be.

THE GRAND MISTRESS [*Still prostrating herself*]

My duties as Grand Mistress make it necessary
for me to call your Majesty's attention to the fact
that this is contrary to the rites. Audiences must
take place in the Throne Room, and be conducted
in accordance with all the rules of immemorial
etiquette.

EMPRESS

We are above all rites and rules. I have spoken
my will.

THE GRAND MISTRESS

The orders of your Majesty shall be transmitted
to the officials of the palace, who will inform the
princes and the dignitaries.

EMPRESS

It is well.
[*The* GRAND MISTRESS *rises and goes out.*]

SCENE V

THE EMPRESS

[*Leaving the flower-garden, she halts before as-*

*cending the marble stair and turns again to the
flowers.*] Guard well, oh, flowers of the morning,
the secret which I have confided to you. Now it
has escaped from my soul! That it may never return, lock it up, oh, flowers, in your blossoms.
[*She mounts several steps*] And you, ancestral
shades, to whom I make this last prayer, Oh! lend
your aid to your daughter, powerless to triumph
over herself. Make my heart invulnerable, since
you have called me to this sovereign mission. Give
me the force to thrust aside all but my noble duty.
Oh, help me to remember only " the brimming cup
of which not a drop must be spilled! "

[*She mounts the stair.*]

SCENE VI

ARROW-BEARER, ATTENDANTS

[*They enter hastily along the path at the foot of
the steps. ARROW-BEARER, raising his head, recog-
nises the EMPRESS, on her way along the Imperial
stair. He makes a sign of warning to those who
follow him, and all terrified throw themselves prostrate, their faces to the ground. As soon as she has
disappeared, ARROW-BEARER makes a sign to the
ATTENDANTS to rise.*]

ARROW-BEARER [*To the* ATTENDANTS]

Put the throne here and set this bench very near, in case the Empress should accord to some privileged one the honour of being seated in her presence. Place these perfumes in the censers that the ladies-in-waiting will only have to light them.

[*Enter the guards, whom he draws up at the foot of the stairs.*]

SCENE VII

The same FAITHFUL PRINCE, MINISTER *and* COMMANDER IN CHIEF. WINGED PRINCE, GENERAL *and* GRAND SECRETARY; POPLAR, *a minister*; VEILED-LIGHT, COUNCILLOR; CHAMBERLAINS, COUNCILLORS, MANDARINS, *etc. They enter in turn. Lastly the* TARTAR EMPEROR *and* FOUNT-IN-THE-FOREST.

POPLAR [*To* FAITHFUL PRINCE]

If your Excellency would say a word for me to the Empress, my desires would be fulfilled and I should obtain the red button, which I have earned by my services.

FAITHFUL

I know your merits and I realise what you deserve. But believe me, true greatness is above titles.

We are devoting our lives to a noble cause, for the joy of seeing it triumph, and not in the hope of a reward. If we die in the service, our name will shine with a brightness, more enduring I assure you, than that of a ruby in the crown of your hat —— However, rest assured I shall do my utmost to obtain it for you, since you aspire to it.

POPLAR

I shall be grateful to you to my dying day.
[*He bows and goes out.*]

WINGED PRINCE [*To* FAITHFUL PRINCE]
May I enquire after your precious health?

FAITHFUL PRINCE [*Bowing*]

How kind of you to trouble about so trifling a matter! My health is good, thank you. I dare to hope that yours, infinitely more precious, is also excellent to the joy of us all.

WINGED PRINCE [*Bowing again*]

You see me overwhelmed by a solicitude of which I am unworthy. Thank you, I am very well. Without excessive pain I am reaching the allotted span — a poor thing, it is true — of my days.

FAITHFUL PRINCE

Did you succeed in seeing the representative of our enemies, the Viceroy of Nanking?

WINGED PRINCE

I saw him and I dictated a report, which he agreed to send to Peking, but I have had to pay dearly for his discretion.

FAITHFUL PRINCE

If only we gain thereby a few days' respite, we shall not need to regret the bait thrown into the mouth of the Tiger. The treasures of the Mings, happily, are far from exhausted and the secret vaults, all unknown to the Tartars, still contain more than is necessary to defray the expenses of war.

[*They go out in conversation*]

VEILED-LIGHT   [*Talking with a* COUNCILLOR]

There is a method of obtaining calabashes of a magnificent red. You graft the young plant with cockscombs ——

COUNCILLOR

With cockscombs? —— Can it be done?

VEILED-LIGHT

Yes, you bury them alongside the roots and pass the stems through the flesh.

A SECRETARY

I know another process for obtaining gourds of celestial blue.

COUNCILLOR   [*To* VEILED LIGHT]
Where did you get your information?

VEILED LIGHT

I read it in the Tu Tien Shan, a work in 20 volumes, containing the most curious secrets of horticulture.

[*They pass on.*]

AN OFFICER

How kind of our Empress to give us audience in the open air, among the flowers!

A STOUT MANDARIN

And to dispense with prostration. At my age and with my figure, the performance is very difficult, and, as you know, one is so easily made to appear ridiculous!

WINGED PRINCE   [*To* FAITHFUL PRINCE, *watching the approach of the* TARTAR EMPEROR *and* FOUNT-IN-THE-FOREST]

I once met the Governor of the South, but I must be confusing him with someone else, for I recollect a person very different from this one. Yet, if I had ever seen those eyes, it seems to me that their expression would have remained in my memory.

FAITHFUL PRINCE

Indeed he has most uncommon expression and an extraordinary dignity.

EMPEROR   [*To* FOUNT]

What makes you so uneasy?

FOUNT   [*In a whisper*]

I am certain that I recognised here in the palace two officers from Peking, disguised, like ourselves.

EMPEROR

Yes? No doubt they were spies sent out in pursuit of me.

FOUNT

I do not think so. More likely the leaders of a conspiracy, against Nanking, perhaps to take it by surprise. We must leave here as soon as possible. All is in readiness, the horses are saddled, the vessel under steam —— You wished to see this palace with your own eyes. You have succeeded, now let us depart.

EMPEROR

Depart before having seen her for a last time? Oh, no. Nothing could make me give up that happiness, which has come to be for me the most desirable thing in the world.

FOUNT

Every minute here we are risking our heads —— At least as soon as you have had your audience, I beg you not to delay another instant.

EMPEROR

You have my promise.

FOUNT

The Faithful Prince has looked toward you several times and you cannot do otherwise now than greet him. He is Prime Minister and Commander-in-Chief, the most important person here; a great heart and a fine character. His rank places him above a viceroy.

EMPEROR

What shall I say to him?

FOUNT

A few polite commonplaces.

EMPEROR

Can I do so? [*He approaches the* FAITHFUL PRINCE *and salutes him.*] Illustrious Prince, may a long and happy life be yours! It is a blessing of Heaven to be permitted to gaze upon your noble countenance and to meet the light of your eyes.

FAITHFUL PRINCE [*Returning the bow*]

In truth I might say the same to you —— But I beg of you let us dispense with compliments. Are you satisfied with your government of the South?

EMPEROR

That region is the most faithfully rebellious of the whole Empire, and is so far away that the orders for its repression are lost before they reach it. The inhabitants refuse to pay the tax levied by the Tartars and of their own accord deposit the money in our coffers.

FAITHFUL PRINCE

You do not fail to accept only half of it, and to refuse it altogether during bad years? ——

EMPEROR

I have done so, which accounts for our popularity.

FAITHFUL PRINCE

Perhaps you would like to be near the throne, in order to obtain a higher rank, more in accordance with your merits. Make use of my influence to support your request ——

EMPEROR

I am the slave of her Majesty, ready to serve her in any position in which she may wish to employ me, but I ask for nothing, and the good opinion which Your Excellence has of my merits is to me the most acceptable recompense.

FAITHFUL PRINCE

I congratulate you on being without ambition and not fixing a prize on your devotion —— Our Sovereign will appear soon.

EMPEROR [*To* FOUNT]

Did I acquit myself creditably?

FOUNT

In very dangerous words. Ah, how I wish I
saw you safely away from here!

EMPEROR

Oh, that I might remain always! —— She is
coming!

SCENE VIII

The same, THE EMPRESS, *in Costume of State*
[*As soon as she appears at the top of the terrace
the perfumes begin to burn in the censers. The
guards unfurl the banners which they are holding in
their hands. Chamberlains and grand equerries
form a line on either side of the staircase, bending
the knee. Before her is carried the yellow umbrella
with three flounces, mounted on a handle bent in the
form of a swan's neck. Behind two* ATTENDANTS
carry tall feather screens, emblems of sovereignty.]
ALL THE ATTENDANTS [*in a low voice, with eyes
lowered*]

Ten thousand years! Ten thousand years! ten
times ten thousand years!

EMPRESS

Happiness be with you, my faithful ones! May
you live many long days! —— [*She descends.*

The FAITHFUL PRINCE *and the* WINGED PRINCE
receive her at the foot of the steps.]

WINGED PRINCE

The flowers grow pale with envy at the approach
of our Sovereign.

FAITHFUL PRINCE

Her presence doubles the brilliancy of the day.
    FOUNT   [*In a whisper to the* EMPEROR]
In truth, she is as beautiful as the pink peony.

EMPEROR

Say rather that the flower is all but as lovely as
she.

EMPRESS [*Stopping on the last steps, between*
PRINCES] There are some hours when nature appears more splendid, the light of Heaven more radiant, when all things of the world seem transfigured
and new, and the soul then expands in the joy of
living —— Oh, my faithful ones despite our
threatening to-morrows, the present is for your Sovereign one of those rare hours. [*In an aside*] It
seems as though I had suddenly become two personalities, a new rapture and unknown hopes fill my
bewildered heart.

EMPEROR [*To* FOUNT]

Her words express what I feel in myself.   Before

this glorious hour I knew not what it meant to live ——

The EMPRESS *advances slowly, stopping to speak a few words to persons bowing before her. To* VEILED-LIGHT *she says*]

You desired the government of the fortress of Tang-Men. The Emperor accords you that title and the appanages which go with it.

VEILED-LIGHT

[*Bending the knee*]   I shall redouble my zeal to be worthy of such an honour.

EMPRESS

Do so.   [*She passes on, while* GRAND EQUERRY *places a scroll of yellow satin in the hand of* VEILED-LIGHT, *who receives it on his knees. To an officer.*]

The Emperor appoints you to that higher rank which you have so deservedly earned.

THE OFFICER

My life belongs to your Majesties, and my sole desire is to be able to sacrifice it in a good cause.

EMPRESS

Keep it for our service.

[*A yellow scroll is given to the officer*]

I offer to each of you a slight gift in assurance of my protection and as a memento of my accession ——

ALL

Ten thousand years, ten thousand times ten thousand years.

[*Pages distribute the gifts.*]

FAITHFUL PRINCE   [*Presenting* POPLAR]

Your devoted servant is ambitious to see the coral button of his hat changed to a ruby.   I venture to support his request to your Majesty.

EMPRESS

Recommended by you, his merit is certain.   I accord the rank with pleasure.

POPLAR

My heart overflows with gratitude.

THE EMPRESS   [*To the* TARTAR EMPEROR]

And you, Prince, do you desire nothing?   Are you too proud to name the favour which would please you?

POPLAR

Nay, I ask one of Heaven, one only, that it will stay the flight of time and prolong this rapturous hour.

EMPRESS   [*At once surprised and somewhat offended, she looks at him a long time, but her gaze becomes tender and she finally smiles.*]   Does that depend on Heaven alone?   [*She takes her place on the throne.*]

HERALD   [*Announcing*]

The Empress commands tea to be served.

ALL

Ten thousand years! ——

[*The cup-bearers serve tea, fruit and cakes.
Each one bends the knee as he takes his cup.*]

The EMPRESS   [*Making a sign to the* TARTAR
EMPEROR, *to be seated on the tabouret, near the
throne*]

Come here Prince. There is also a present for
you.

A GRAND SECRETARY   [*In a whisper to a* COUN-
CILLOR]   With one word she has made him Prince,
and now she permits him to be seated in her presence!

COUNCILLOR

He does not seem at all surprised at the honour.

GRAND SECRETARY

He is the favourite of to-morrow. We shall
have to reckon with him.

EMPRESS

You gave my son a jewel marvellously cut, a
dragon, emblem of the Imperial Power. He is de-
lighted with it, and wishes me to offer you in his
name, the emblem of the Empresses, a phœnix, with
wings of sapphires and rubies.

[GOLDEN LOTUS *approaches and presents a jewel-case on a salver*]

EMPEROR

I wish to receive it on bended knee, and to assure you that it will be with me always.   [*He bends the knee.*]

EMPRESS   [*To* GOLDEN LOTUS]

Golden Lotus, did you, as I command, attach a ring on which to hang it?

GOLDEN LOTUS

Yes, Your Majesty.

EMPEROR

Until to-day I had seen but the nests of ordinary birds, and I did not believe in that incomparable bird the Phœnix.   It is only to-day that its existence was disclosed to me by the evidence of my enchanted eyes.   [*He hangs the jewel on his belt.*]

EMPRESS

Alas, the phœnix and the dragon are dragged down by chains to-day, and cannot reach the heights to which they aspire in the clouds.

EMPEROR

Ah, how ardently I wish I were the Tartar Emperor reigning at Peking!

Empress

What a strange and dismal idea! You wish you were my mortal enemy? Why?

Emperor

That I might attempt to set all China at your feet, to bring to you your own, and then to be your most faithful subject.

Empress   [*Smiling*]

What a dream! —— But from that Emperor I could accept nothing —— nothing, but death. Do not desire to be anyone else than you are for no one has ever inspired in me so sudden and deep a sympathy. Do not leave the palace yet —— Await my commands. Since you have no ambition I must have it in your place, and keep you perhaps more near to me —— Farewell until we meet!

Emperor   [*Rising and bowing*]

Whether near or far, my thoughts will ever be prostrated at the feet of your Majesty.

[*He goes, on his way saying in a whisper to* Fount] Friend, in my disguise, I triumph! For the first time for three hundred years a Chinese woman has given her love to a Tartar!

Fount

Carry away with you your glorious joy; but I beg you, let us depart at once.

[*Tea is offered to the* EMPEROR. *Gradually he slips away, led by his* MINISTERS]

THE COUNCILLOR [*To a* SECRETARY]

He did not even bend the knee to receive the Imperial tea.

SECRETARY

He understands that to him already all is permitted.

EMPRESS. [*In an aside, dreamily*]

I am no longer mistress of my will —— The words fly from my lips, like captive birds escaped and making for the sky —— I have betrayed myself —— with happiness.

[*Uproar and cries, all the attendants in alarm. Officials of the Palace enter hurriedly, their hands on their sabres.* FAITHFUL PRINCE *and* WINGED PRINCE *approach to defend the* EMPRESS, *who has risen from her throne.*]

SCENE IX

The same except the EMPEROR *and* FOUNT. PALACE OFFICIALS, ARROW-BEARER.

EMPRESS

What has happened?

OFFICER

A conspiracy.

ANOTHER

It has failed!

ARROW-BEARER   [*Kneeling*]

Our young Emperor is safe.

EMPRESS [*Crying aloud*]

My son!—— It was against my son!——
Where is my son?

SCENE X

The same. THE CHILD *with his* NURSES *and*
GUARDS.

THE CHILD   [*Running to his mother and kneeling before her*]

Here I am, mother.

EMPRESS

Ah!   [*She arises and embraces him.*]   Now I
can control myself to listen —— Speak!

ARROW-BEARER

Divine Sovereign, two Tartar spies entered the
palace with the monstrous design of kidnapping our
young Emperor.   Like tigers they lay in wait, hidden in the bushes.   They came out all unawares and

dared to lay a hand on the sacred person of your son.

The Child

Mother they threw a cloth over my head and tightened it round my throat.

Empress

Oh!

The Child

I could not cry out, but I struggled hard. Oh! I am very strong, I am ——

Arrow-Bearer

We were on guard. The nurses with cries of horror called for our aid. We ran to them and seized the criminals.

Empress

Ah, you have them? Let them be brought here at once.

[Arrow-Bearer *rises and goes out. The* Empress *seats herself again.*]

Winged Prince

Their trial will not take long.

Faithful Prince

Heaven was watching over its young son and saved him.

ALL

Ten thousand years, ten thousand times ten thousand years.

SCENE XI.

The same. TWO SPIES, *their hands tied, each one held by two guards. They are thrown on to their knees at the foot of the throne.*

WINGED PRINCE

Who are you?

FIRST SPY

Faithful servants of the dynasty of the Tsing.

WINGED PRINCE

Where do you come from?

SECOND SPY

From the only capital of our great and pure Empire.

WINGED PRINCE

Your crime is flagrant and needs no further proof, what have you to say?

FIRST SPY

Nothing.

Second Spy

Yes! We wished to kidnap the child, to hold him as a hostage and thus to have you at our mercy. We have nothing further to say. Our lips are sealed.

Winged Prince

Name your accomplices.

Second Spy

We shall say nothing.

Winged Prince

Ha! ha! We have made others speak. [*To the* Empress] The torture at once, is it not?

Empress

Torture, no! Death, instant death.

Faithful Prince [*To the* Empress]

I venture to suggest to your Majesty that it might be better perhaps to imprison these men in a dungeon. We do not know who they are, nor of how great importance in the eyes of the enemy. What secrets might we not indeed extract from these two! ——

Empress

What! After what they have done, you would have them see the light of another day? —— Remember that they have dared to lay a hand on the sacred person of him in whom lives all our hope; they have bruised his neck, frail as a stem of a flower. To kidnap him as hostage, they said! How do I know that they did not rather mean to kill my child.

ALL

Death! Death!

EMPRESS

Yes, death! And have them thrown to the beasts that eat dead bodies. Their graves will be the maws of crows and dogs. At once!

[*The* FAITHFUL PRINCE *gives a signal, and the condemned prisoners are lifted to their feet.*]

FIRST SPY

We have risked our lives. We have lost and we accept death.

SECOND SPY

We shall be soon avenged by the great army which is marching against you. To-morrow it will be before your walls.

ALL

Death! Death!
[*The condemned men are led away.*]

SCENE XII

The same, except the SPIES, *'A. B., and* THE GUARDS.

EMPRESS   [*To the* CHILD]

Oh, my best beloved! Oh, you, who bear the
sweet name of Son of Springtime, how near was I
to losing you!

THE CHILD

Tell me, mother are those men to be put to
death?

EMPRESS

That is the lightest punishment which their crime
deserves.

THE CHILD

No, it is too much, as they did not kill me.

EMPRESS

But they desired your death. The sentence is too
lenient. And see, I spared them the torture-cham-
ber —— Now, I shall never again dare to be away
from you. No, not even for a minute, my priceless
jewel, shall you again be out of my sight.

FAITHFUL PRINCE

My Sovereign, how it pains me to be forced to
tear your heart by telling you what we believe to be
your painful duty, we to whose advice your Majesty
deigns to listen. For many days, we have been

resolved to speak, and yet we shrank from the ungrateful task.   But to-day the danger is too pressing.

EMPRESS

Oh, what are you going to say?   [*She descends from her throne.*]

FAITHFUL PRINCE

Alas, that my words shall be like the cold north wind which kills the flowers.

EMPRESS

I already feel the chill in my very soul.

FAITHFUL PRINCE

You must for a time be separated from your son.

EMPRESS

[*With drooping head*]   I knew too well!

FAITHFUL PRINCE

The hope of all, THE VICTORY to come, our Young Emperor!— He should be protected from the dangers of war, in safety, far from here, in some inaccessible province.

EMPRESS

"Let the precious torch which shall illumine the future be placed beyond the reach of the wind."   Thus spoke the astrologer.   Yes, the blind man did see

into the invisible.   Thus is the mystery of his words
explained ——!

FAITHFUL PRINCE

We must obey the oracle.   Misfortune foreseen
can often be avoided.   Winged Prince, and you
Veiled-Light, sage councillors, does your opinion
coincide with mine.

WINGED PRINCE

It is the same in every point.

FAITHFUL PRINCE

And all you, noble chiefs, wise men of letters,
dignitaries, are you too of the opinion that we must
send the young Emperor away.   [*All nod their
heads affirmatively without speaking.*]   And not to-
morrow, not even this evening alas — for each moment the danger increases ——   We must act at
once, if your Majesty consents to the sacrifice.

EMPRESS

Oh!   You place me in a circle of fire, which you
narrow again and again, far too quickly.   But
where are the Tartar armies, now?   Not yet beneath our walls, surely.   We are not besieged!
The roads are still open ——   [*She presses her son
to her breast.*]   Leave him with me just another
day, at least give me time to find the necessary
strength to bear this new affliction ——   I am the

Empress, yes, but I am also a mother —— One does not take a child from its mother as one plucks a flower from its stem —— Wait! ——

FAITHFUL PRINCE

Wait, my Sovereign! But will not your despair be infinitely more intense should harm come to his Majesty because of a weak tenderness? Think of the turmoil of a siege, the horror and the risk of battle! Let us thank Heaven for giving us time to place our young Master in safety. As soon as the danger is over, he will return to you.

EMPRESS

Oh, do not speak of return to lessen my distress, as you would comfort a child! —— Let us not talk of the future, which is black and cloudy —— But Wisdom has spoken, and my rebellion is over. I shall have the strength to submit. [*To the child, whom she holds still pressed close against her.*] My son, you must go away from me for a little while —— Ah, tears fill my eyes at the idea. But when I think of keeping you in this palace, in the midst of such terrible dangers, anguish crushes my heart —— My best beloved, you must go.

THE CHILD [*Embracing her*]

What! I must go on account of the Tartars? Well, I am not afraid, I am not really. Do you

think that I am afraid? You remain here, my
mother, and where you remain there I must be too.
—— Leave my mother on account of the Tartars?
I do not want to! You all hear me. I do not want
to.

EMPRESS

My son! You will show greater courage in saying good-bye to me. And you must prove yourself
worthy of your noble, your more than human lot.
Remember that you are not an ordinary child.
Under your delicate flesh, in the fine network of
your veins, flows the blood of divinity. The Bright
Dynasty has no representative but you alone. Oh,
my best beloved! You are the son of Heaven!

[THE CHILD, *very thoughtful, lets his head sink*]

FAITHFUL PRINCE

Raise up your face, do not turn it down, dazzled
by the bright name of your ancestors. Already you
must be master of your feelings. You owe your
heart as a debt to this people unnumbered, which is
conquered and oppressed and looks to you for its
deliverance. To this people alone belong your
thoughts, your actions, your very life.

THE CHILD   [*Sad and grave*]

I will go —— I will not cry.

EMPRESS

To whom shall we entrust this greatest of our treasures? You have no doubt thought about it. I feel that your plans are made.

FAITHFUL PRINCE

Our young Emperor has shown without knowing him, a sympathy for the Viceroy of the South. Now he is precisely the best situated to offer him an inviolable refuge. My advice is that we entrust him to him.

EMPRESS   [*To* THE CHILD]

Will that please you?

THE CHILD

Yes.

EMPRESS

It was also my idea. The Viceroy is certainly still at the palace awaiting my orders.   [*To* ARROW-BEARER]   Call him here.

[ARROW-BEARER *goes out.*]

FAITHFUL PRINCE   [*To the* NURSES]

Prepare for an immediate departure. You will not leave your young master.

EMPRESS   [*To* THE CHILD]

I envy them.   Would that I were to-day only your servant.

FAITHFUL PRINCE [*To the* GUARDS]

An escort of five hundred men, well chosen and fully armed. [*Exit* THE GUARD] *To* WINGED PRINCE.] Prince, you will accompany the Emperor, and as soon as he is in safety you will return to take your place here among us.

WINGED PRINCE

I shall prove myself worthy of your trust, my preparations will be brief. [*He goes out.*]

To your posts now, noble defenders of the Son of Heaven. We are always ready for war, I know it. But let us make ourselves still stronger. Let us brace up our courage, let us prepare our hearts —— Let messengers be sent out at once to discover exactly the position and importance of the army which is marching against us. [*The* EMPRESS *gives a signal*] You may take your leave.

[THE SOLDIERS *go out one after another, with a genuflection.*]

EMPRESS [*To* THE CHILD]

I gaze upon you to engrave on my memory your adorable features. I fill my eyes with them, just as if I did not already know every detail, every line; but they are going from me —— I would wish to have them carved in marble, and memory is as unstable as water.

SCENE XIII

The same, WINGED PRINCE *returns hurriedly.*
  WINGED PRINCE   [*To* FAITHFUL PRINCE.]
A courier has just arrived and brings strange
news.

EMPRESS
What is it now?

WINGED PRINCE
The Viceroy of the South sends to explain to your
Majesty that the reason that he was unable to reach
the palace for the ceremony to which he was invited
was because he was taken prisoner at the moment
when he was about to enter Nanking.

EMPRESS
But the Viceroy came here!

WINGED PRINCE
That was not the real Viceroy.

EMPRESS
Not the real Viceroy?

WINGED PRINCE
He was imprisoned on a ship, but no harm came

to him, and he was treated with every consideration
—— His letter explains how he escaped.

FAITHFUL PRINCE

Treated with every consideration! What does
that imply? The spies of the Tsings are less generous.

WINGED PRINCE

The Viceroy sent this courier in all haste; he
awaits orders to come and prostrate himself at
the foot of the throne and sue for pardon.

EMPRESS

Then that man who was here? —— Oh, in what
frightful web are we now caught? —— And I
was about to entrust my son to that unknown man!
—— I ordered him to remain here. Run, perhaps he has not yet gone.

ARROW-BEARER [*Returning*]

The pavilion is empty. This silk scroll was
placed so as to attract immediate attention.

EMPRESS [*excitedly*]

Give it to me! —— [ARROW-BEARER *gives the
scroll to* FAITHFUL PRINCE, *who gives it to the* EM-
PRESS. *Aside.*] In my dream —— The serpent

that coiled about me —— Ah! It was he! [*She steps aside to read.*] Verses! —— In my trouble, I shall scarce be able to read them. And then the meaning seems so mysterious. [*To* THE OFFICERS *standing nearest to her.*] Let twenty horsemen be sent out at once in all directions, pursue him. Let the neighbouring towns be searched as well. A hundred thousand taels to him who brings that man back to me. Go! [*To* FAITHFUL PRINCE *handing him the silken scroll.*] Read it to me Faithful Prince.

FAITHFUL PRINCE [*reading*]

Beneath my mask I kept a secret watch on you.
 You saw my face, but not my features true;
You heard my words, but not my secret heart.
  The day will come when I shall throw away the
    mask,
  Play your good angel's part,
And all shall bow beneath the conquering dragon's
    task.
 The traitor is a fine scholar, but he does not un-
mask his identity.

WINGED PRINCE [*To* THE CHILD]

Your Majesty must no longer keep about your neck like a relic a present given you by an impostor.

THE CHILD [*Excitedly*] But I will keep it. I

thought of my dead father when I saw that man, and when he told me that he would like to have me for a son, he was keeping back his tears.

EMPRESS

The instinct of children does not mislead them —— nor can I believe, either, that the unknown visitor meant us harm —— Let us wait awhile before we begin to hate him.

[*She stretches out her hand and takes the poem which she places next to her heart.*]

SCENE XIV

The Same. THE WOMEN, *and* ARROW-BEARER FIRST NURSE

All the preparations are completed.

ARROW-BEARER

The escort is ready.

EMPRESS   [*Embracing her son*]

Yes, but to whom will you now entrust your Emperor?   Let us take time to think at least —— Or perhaps, since there is such immediate need, you have deceived me, and we are surrounded?   Where is the Tartar army?   I am not an idol shut up in a shrine.   Let me be told the truth! —— Where is this army?

Faithful Prince

Very near and in great force —— The messengers will bring us details this evening —— In order not to cloud the brow of your Majesty during the glorious days of your investiture we have deceived you it is true. Forgive us!

Empress

I understand —— but now my son, to whom is he to be entrusted?

Faithful Prince

Still to the Viceroy of the South to the real one we may trust him. His devotion of ten years has stood all tests. So we must now march to meet him, and without losing an hour he must retrace his steps toward Yunnan with his precious charge. To this end the start must be made instantly, so that the two escorts may meet before nightfall. [*To* Winged Prince] Prince, until further orders, remain with the Emperor. Keep up constant communication with the frontier, and on the first alarm take the child out of the Empire.

Empress

And every day a courier must bring me news, as long as the roads are free about our walls and our gates are open.

Winged Prince

I shall attend to all, relying on none other than myself.

Faithful Prince

And we all know the value of your watchfulness. [*One of the officers who left previously at the command of the* Empress *returns hastily.*]

Officer

The horsemen have returned —— The fugitives have been seen, the man and his accomplice. They were riding horses which devoured the ground. One of those swift ships such as are used by the Western Barbarian was awaiting them at the water's edge. It is bearing them along at present with the speed of lightning. All pursuit would be futile.

Empress

I was prepared for that —— He would not permit himself to be captured like an ordinary fugitive! —— No, I knew that he would carry away with him the mystery which he was pleased to keep up here.

Faithful Prince [*To* The Empress.]

Your Majesty, the time has come, we must hasten.

EMPRESS

Yes, I am ready —— Only one instant, one last minute! [*She conducts the little* EMPEROR *to the throne, on which she seats him.*] Permit me to render to the Son of Heaven the homage which is his due. [*She kneels.*] May your life be happy and long, your reign peaceful and prosperous! [*She bows three times.*] May your dynasty endure eternally.

[*The men and the nurses prostrate themselves.*]

THE CHILD [*on the verge of tears*]

I promised that I would not cry.

EMPRESS

In triumph and glory may you come back to us soon! [*She rises.* THE CHILD *descends from the throne, approaches the* EMPRESS, *and kneels in turn*]

THE CHILD

Mother, tell me, I am not going for long, am I?

EMPRESS [*Stooping and embracing her son passionately*] No, my best beloved, no —— only for a few days if the gods whom I implore will it so! —— Have courage sweet little flower —— [*To the* NURSES] Now go!

[*The* NURSES *lead away the little* EMPEROR. *He*

keeps his gaze fixed on his mother until he is out of sight.]

SCENE XV

The EMPRESS, *the* FAITHFUL PRINCE, *and several* LADIES-IN-WAITING.

[THE EMPRESS *watches him disappear, and then mounts the steps of the terrace to get a last glimpse of him, and when he is out of sight she cries aloud in her anguish, wringing her hands.*]

FAITHFUL PRINCE
Noble Sovereign, have courage.

EMPRESS
Ah, no, leave me.   I am at the end of my strength!
—— I played the Empress, did I not, as long as my child was here? —— Now that he is gone, let me be a woman, let me be his mother! —— I shall never again see him whom you have just taken away from me.   Never, do you hear?   I feel it, I know it!   Since we are above ordinary beings, may Heaven be just to us and give us superhuman strength!   Why have we hearts like other people, and anguish which breaks them? —— Ah,! the very beggar-women in rags in the street are less miserable!   No handsome spy comes to them, to make

their souls falter, and then flees —— and after that their children are not taken away from them! —— Your Empress would rather be a beggar, hungry and cold, but clasping her little one to her breast —— Yes, a beggar I tell you, who holds out her hand to passers-by as she sits on the steps of a temple! ——[*Sobbing, she throws herself on the terrace steps.*]

CURTAIN

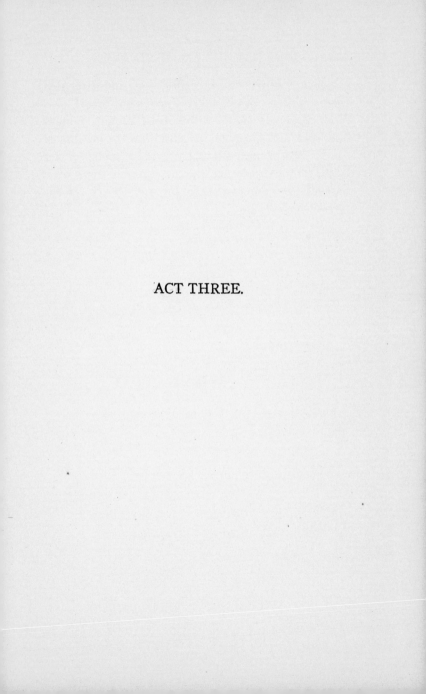

ACT THREE.

[*Before the curtain rises, shots are heard. It is night-fall in the Imperial Citadel at Nanking, half battered-down by the* TARTARS. *Behind a huge wall with battlements are heard the sound of trumpets and the shouts of soldiers in the distance. At the back, to the left, is a bronze gate, heavily boarded and surmounted by a black turret with a three-tiered angular roof. In the middle of the stage is a funeral pile of scaffolding and fagots. At the back, to the right, the crenellated wall continues; terraces are visible and in the far distance the outline of the palace stands out in relief against the sky, yellow in the setting sun. On the top of the wall, and over the gateway are Chinese soldiers, who are firing their last shots at the invisible besiegers.*]

SCENE I

The EMPRESS, *the* FAITHFUL PRINCE, ARROW-BEARER, the LADIES-IN-WAITING, CHINESE SOLDIERS.

[*Wounded men are lying in their own blood here and there among the ruins. The* EMPRESS *is in the middle of the stage, accoutred like a warrior, helmeted, holding a weapon in her bleeding hand. The* FAITHFUL PRINCE *is on the top of the rampart with the* SOLDIERS. ARROW-BEARER, *mortally wounded, lies in the foreground to the left.*]

FAITHFUL PRINCE [*From the height of the ramparts giving orders to cease fire*] Enough,, my brave friends!—— Stop shooting down the fugitives—— Let us keep our powder for the final attack.

[*The soldiers cease firing.*]

They have fled, once again we are saved!——

EMPRESS

Ah! Saved, yes!—— Saved for a few minutes at least. We have time to meditate before death. [*She sits on a stone. To the* LADIES-IN-WAITING *who flock about her.*] Look now to those who are suffering. I need nothing, only my hand is bleeding, that does not matter—— See what they need, go to their aid; you have the poison in the tiny flasks, have you not?

LADIES-IN-WAITING

[*Showing her the golden flasks which they carry in the folds of their dress, on to each of which is attached a little cup of jade.*] We have them, noble Sovereign.

EMPRESS

That which they most desire, no doubt, is death —— Pour out the draught of the Great Deliverance for those who are suffering the most —— Be sparing with it, however, for, alas! we have not enough for all. The contents of the little cup of jade chained to the flask is sufficient for one man, it is the proper dose. Go, my devoted maids, bring them sleep. That is your duty in this hour. [*To* CINNAMON.] And you, Cinnamon, remain near me, you shall pour out my portion —— Place your flask on the stone, very near me, with my Imperial cup.

[CINNAMON *obeys. The other* LADIES-IN-WAITING *go among the wounded, leaning over them and offering them the potion in a low voice. In the distance firing is still heard.*]

GOLDEN LOTUS

[*Very gently to* ARROW-BEARER, *whom she approaches at once*]
My lord, do you wish to die? Then I shall empty

the cup also soon after you —— Do you wish to die?

ARROW-BEARER [*After a silence and as if in a trance*]

No, my fair trembling flower, my fair flower of the lake! —— Before you came to me, I wished it —— Now I wish it no longer. Let me remain for a little while among the living, to cherish in my heart that word of love which you have just spoken. Help those who are suffering more than I, without a friend —— and then you will return and I shall rest my head on your knees before going to the Land of the Shades.

GOLDEN LOTUS

It shall be as you command, dear lord —— Be sure I will return to you.

[*She goes to the assistance of the other wounded, followed by the gaze of the dying* ARROW-BEARER. *The soldiers in the foreground add beams, fagots, and branches to the funeral pile. A tumult is heard to the right, in the wings, where more soldiers come on.*]

EMPRESS

Who is there?

CAPTAIN OF SOLDIERS

It is our envoy Wan-tsi who has succeeded in approaching our walls and will bring us the news from without.   We have thrown down the rope-ladder to him, and here he is.

EMPRESS

Ah! —— Let him come.   [*To the soldiers who stand behind her and are adding to the fire.*]   Rest awhile my friends!   There is more than enough now to consume my body —— Why do you make the fire so large?

CAPTAIN

Why do we want so large a fire? —— Faithful Prince will tell your Majesty, when he presents our last request.

SCENE II

The same, with the ENVOY WAN-TSI, *who approaches the* EMPRESS.   *His shoes and the hem of his robe are blood-stained.   He prostrates himself.*

EMPRESS

Arise, we have no further need of prostrations. We are all equal here.   There is but one rank now, that which is conferred on all alike by the nobility of sacrifice.   [WAN-TSI *rises.*]   Now, speak —— spare me nothing —— Besides I guess ——

WAN-TSI

Ah, yes, all is over, Oh, my Sovereign. Only your Palace still stands.

EMPRESS

But not for long!

WAN-TSI

The approaches to the walls have been abandoned. Perchance they may permit us to live until to-night has ended.

EMPRESS

And the rest of the city, the western citadels?

WAN-TSI

Are in the hands of the Tartars. All alike! —— This cast off uniform of some enemy saved me —— In the streets they are burning, killing, and murdering. Several thousand women have succeeded in throwing themselves into the river —— The others have been outraged, and strangled at the same time. Blood flows along the pavement in streams like the water of Heaven after a storm. Every gutter discharges itself in the river like a great red fan. Down the whole length of the street corpses are to be seen, their bodies still warm, pouring blood through the gashes in their throats —— Noble Sovereign, on my way I climbed over thousands of dead bodies, my feet became entangled in their long hair trailing from the several heads —— Oh Majesty, it is the end. [*He kneels again.*] And now forgive me for being the messenger of misfortune.

EMPRESS

My brave and faithful messenger, I thank you! Arise, I told you, and take your place among my last remaining soldiers ——

[WAN-STI *rises and takes his place among the soldiers, who still continue to add fuel to the fire. To* CINNAMON, *pointing to the flask and the golden cup.*]

Cinnamon, the hour has come.

CINNAMON

Oh Majesty, not yet. [*The other* LADIES-IN-WAITING, *scattered among the wounded, have heard the command and silently come and take their places about their* SOVEREIGN.]

EMPRESS

Would you wish to have them take me alive? That man who has seen, you have beard what he has just said.

TRANQUIL BEAUTY

But the palace is still standing.

PEARL

The army of the South may come to save us.

EMPRESS

To avenge us perhaps —— later. But to save us
—— child, who think you could save us? [*To herself.*] Ah, that mysterious aid for which I have so
foolishly hoped! —— " The Star," said the handsome lying spy, " the star which shall watch over me
so well when all shall bow before the triumph of the
Dragon." Child, who think you could save us?
—— We have no more powder, no more men, no
water, nothing. We have hurled down the stones
of our ramparts; the gates give way, the walls are
crumbling —— [*To* CINNAMON] Give it to me,
the hour has come.

TRANQUIL BEAUTY

Sometimes when one believes all lost, fortune
changes.

PEARL

Beloved sovereign, hasten not the irretrievable.

EMPRESS

The irretrievable would be to wait too long!
[*She makes an imperious sign to* CINNAMON,
*who pours the poison into the cup. But an uproar
is heard from the summit of the rampart to which*

the FAITHFUL PRINCE *has just mounted again above the barricaded gate. Night continues to fall*]

What is it now?

FAITHFUL PRINCE

A small body of Tartars has boldly come unarmed to the very foot of the walls.   One of them, whose manner is calm and noble, says that he has been sent by the Emperor with a last communication to your Majesty.   He showed us, under the light of a torch which we lit, the Imperial seal of the Tsings, of a scroll of yellow silk.

EMPRESS

A communication?   From the usurper to your Sovereign, a communication?   Is not the very idea an insult?   Let these bold men go away unharmed, but tell them to go at once.

[CINNAMON *gradually retires with her cup of poison.*]

FAITHFUL PRINCE   [*Descending again from the ramparts and approaching the* EMPRESS *with an air of mystery.*]   The one whose bearing is so dignified, I seem to have seen before.

EMPRESS

To have seen him.   Where?

Faithful Prince

[*Coming nearer and lowering his voice*] My sovereign, I think —— that unknown, who came the day of the investiture —— I am sure of it — It is he!

Empress

[*Arising bewildered*] Why do you whisper? —— Prince, you almost insult me with that tone of confidence, when it concerns that man. You mean him who presented himself fraudulently as our Viceroy of the South?

Faithful Prince

Yes.

Empress

Very well then, have him brought here. Throw the rope-ladder to him that he may appear before me. [*The ladder is thrown from the top of the wall.*]

Hide the poison, Cinnamon, and the golden flask as well. He who is coming need not know. . . . Has the fire darkened my face?

[*The newcomers appear at the top of the rampart, the* Tartar Emperor *first, followed by* Fount-in-the-Forest *and three other persons in Tartar soldiers' uniform, but unarmed.*]

SCENE III

The Tartar Emperor *and* The Empress

[*The* Emperor *advances while the four men of his suite remain in the rear. At a signal from the* Empress, *the* Ladies-in-Waiting *and all others on the stage retire to the back.*]

EMPEROR

[*Bending the knee before her, as on the Coronation day*]   Oh, Sovereign, oh, brave warrior, may the day dawn which will brighten your dark destiny! [*He rises.*]

EMPRESS   [*Trembling*]

Oh, dispense with all vain formalities.   The minutes left to us are sparingly numbered —— Drop the mask and speak quickly.   Who are you?   A Tartar, alas! are you not?   Otherwise you would have been unable to break through their ring of steel —— A Tartar, say?

EMPEROR

Yes.

EMPRESS

A spy, then, when you came on my Coronation day?   Nothing but a spy, alas!

EMPEROR

No! One who risked his life that day, as he does again, to save yours.

EMPRESS

My life is no longer of any importance, and the right to save it belongs to none. At the Court of the Usurper who reigns at Peking what position is yours?—— Secret agent for venturesome missions? No, a great dignitary, then? Tell me.

EMPEROR

Yes.

EMPRESS

And a Prince?

EMPEROR

What matters it what I am? Your Majesty is the chief concern. Deign to listen to what the Emperor——

EMPRESS   [*Interrupting*]

Where is your Emperor? At the head of his troops?

EMPEROR   [*Embarrassed*]

Well—— No, in his place over yonder. The

rites, I need scarcely tell you, do not permit him to leave it.

[Throughout this dialogue the cannon is heard incessantly in distant parts of the city.]

EMPRESS

The rites, ah, the rites! You see what attention I have paid to the rites, I, the daughter of the Mings, the daughter of Heaven and the Invisible —— I am here in the midst of my soldiers. I am fighting like them! —— And it is he, your phantom Emperor, who dares to send me a message?

EMPEROR

With a message of pardon one always dares ——

EMPRESS

Say rather that a message of pardon is the last message which may be sent when it is from him and concerns me! —— So the Tartars dare to offer pardon! —— You have just passed through my city of Nanking and you have seen? It is glorious, is it not, their work? ——

EMPEROR

Alas! yes, I have seen with horror,—— but I can swear to you by my life that such were not the orders which were given by my Sovereign.

EMPRESS

Ah! a Sovereign then, who has not the force

wherewith to command obedience!—— So others have told me that before —— I still hate him with that ineradicable race-hatred which you know, to which now contempt is added. Oh, that Emperor who smokes opium in his mummy's palace, while his hordes of soldiers at their own free will go through the provinces, leaving red tracks behind and charnel-houses for the vultures!

And if the impossible were to happen and I were to humiliate myself sufficiently to accept his pardon, who would warrant me after all — since he is not obeyed? Amid that army of wild beasts which was here awhile ago and will return soon to shout for our death, who could enforce the order of pardon of your phantom Emperor?—— Who, I ask?

EMPEROR

I!

EMPRESS

You! [*More gently and in some agitation.*] You! Perhaps in very truth you might, for you seem to be one of those whom one dare not disobey. Moreover you have the superb audacity to reappear at this moment! But if the loyalty which I read in your eyes does not deceive me, cease the game which you are playing, and this time answer —— Who are you?

EMPEROR

Who am I? Up to now nothing! Inexistent as a vaporous cloud! Nothing! But to-morrow perhaps everything, if you so wish it. To-morrow everything and radiating at your side like a sun in the blue ether ——

EMPRESS [*Drawing back*]

Ah, you remember all too well my recent indulgence toward your enigmas. Amid the perfume of incense, amid pomp and luxury, I betrayed the weakness of a woman. To-day, no; you find me stronger and more stern, precisely because I am defeated, and know that I must die.

EMPEROR [*Bowing before her*]

Oh, Sovereign, never were you more sacred to me —— Do not be offended by my words and for a short time still allow me my mask and my mystery. Hear only this: A fortnight ago, when I left that palace where I saw you in all your Imperial splendour, I hastened to Peking to request of that Emperor whom you hate that he would stop this horrible war. On the way I learned that our Tartar armies were marching with lightning speed, and I turned back as quick as my ship and horses could take me, to give to them myself the order for peace. I have the right to do so. See, here is the seal which gives me full power in the name of Tsings.

As you have said, I am one of those whom men dare not disobey; at least, not face to face, when I speak —— I have learned now how to give orders and to enforce them. Deign only to allow your soldiers to give the signal for a truce, just to hoist the flag on the tower, and not one of their heads shall fall, I swear it ——

EMPRESS

To make that offer to me, Prince, you must not be of the Imperial blood —— The Daughter of Heaven can never accept the mercy of a Tartar! ——

SCENE IV.

The same, FAITHFUL PRINCE, A WATCHMAN, *the* CAPTAIN *of the* SOLDIERS, *and the* SOLDIERS.

WATCHMAN

[*Announcing from the height of a turret at the summit of the ramparts*]   An army, see, over there. The Tartars are returning! Thousands and thousands of them.   In the distance they appear in the twilight like a long black trail ——

FAITHFUL PRINCE

How far?

WATCHMAN

At the bend of the river, I can see their vanguard —— They are marching along the avenue of Sitche-Men.

FAITHFUL PRINCE

Let them come —— It will be their last attack —— Only at the bend of the river. Then we have still half an hour ——

WATCHMAN

They are lighting their torches, and now I hear their war-trumpets.

FAITHFUL PRINCE

Be it so! —— We shall be ready.

EMPEROR   [*Imploring her with clasped hands*] Sovereign!

The EMPRESS   [*As though ready to yield*]
For myself, no! —— I have declared my intentions, that is my last word! —— [*Pointing to her* SOLDIERS.] But all these brave men, who are ready to drop with exhaustion, with hunger and thirst —— [*To* FAITHFUL PRINCE] Ah, well, for their sakes, yes, let us raise the flag of truce.

FAITHFUL PRINCE   [*Incredulously*]
The flag of truce!

EMPRESS

Yes, I have said so, oh, noble subject! I have said it!—— My death alone must be sufficient satisfaction for the enemy. Since there is no more hope, of what avail is this final slaughter? Let the signal be raised.

FAITHFUL PRINCE

Not one of the warriors will yield.

EMPRESS

But if I command them!—— Am I no longer their Empress?

FAITHFUL PRINCE

Submissive to your every command, they refuse to obey that one order.

EMPRESS   [*To her* SOLDIERS]

Can it be true?—— My friends, this instant I command it, do you hear me?—— Oh, spare me this excess of anguish, my dear rebels!—— You cannot wish that I should be transported into the other world along the stream of your blood——

[*The* SOLDIERS *drop their heads and stand motionless, holding their weapons.*]

CAPTAIN OF SOLDIERS.   [*After a silence*]

Majesty, the Prince has already answered for all

of us! We emphatically refuse to ask for a truce.

EMPRESS   [*Turning towards the* EMPEROR *in a sudden exultation of triumph.*]   Ah, you see I am like your Tartar Emperor; I am not obeyed.   Go tell him, report to your master —— and at the same time you may tell him that we know how to die nobly in the palace of the Mings.   Go, my lord, you may take your leave.

EMPEROR   [*Imploring more insistently*]

Sovereign, what if I now were to implore your pardon —— the right to remain here and die at your side?

EMPRESS

I grant the honour of dying at the side of the Empress, only to those brave men — who are of my race, do you understand? —— and who have spilled their blood to defend me.   Go, my lord, I have commanded you.

[*Coming toward him, speaking very low and quickly, like a desperate woman.*]   One more word, however —— My son, who is still in the keeping of the army of the South —— My son —— since you seem to dare all and to have all power will you try to save him? —— But no —— when it is the mother who speaks in me I can no longer reason —— To attempt that would mean to be a traitor to the master whom you serve ——

Emperor

I serve no master, I am above treason, free as the gods, and answerable to my own conscience only. I will try —— I will live to try.

Empress

Do so, and be this your reward —— Later, among the clouds, where all the dead meet and are at peace —— my shades shall not be hostile to yours —— Now go, my lord, our last moments are necessary to us —— [*To* Faiithful Prince, *making a sign to him to conduct the* Tartar Emperor.] Prince, the audience is at an end.

Faithful Prince

[*To the* Emperor, *who hesitates, as if on the point of making a decisive revelation*] Go, my lord. You have heard our sovereign dismiss you.

[*He wants to lead him to that part of the wall where he ascended*]

Empress. [*Indicating the bronze gate, barricaded by boards*] No, open that gate. We still have time. For the last time, I desire that my palace be left as if I still had liberty and power —— Open it. [*The* Soldiers *hasten to take away the boards and open the two doors of the gateway.*] All honour must be accorded the messenger of peace.

[*The* SOLDIERS *kneel, the gong and the trumpets are sounded.*]

EMPEROR

Yes, messenger of peace, in spite of you yourself and in all circumstance. [*Turning about, facing her and speaking like one inspired.*] The dragon will descend from the height of the dark storm clouds —— and in his claws he will gently pick up, in her own despite, the beautiful phœnix who wished to die ——

[*He goes out, followed by the four* TARTAR *warriors. The* SOLDIERS *barricade the gate again with planks and stones.*]

SCENE V.

The same, without the EMPEROR *and the* TAR-TARS.

The EMPRESS, [*as the* LADIES-IN-WAITING *gather about her.*] Who is that man —— who is so like a god?

PEARL

All of a tremble, we watched him from afar ——

TRANQUIL BEAUTY

His eyes radiated noble love.

CINNAMON

Yet your Majesty, always so gentle to us, seemed very haughty towards him.

EMPRESS. [*Without replying, dreamily repeats the Coronation admonition.*] Be attentive and anxious as if you carried a vase filled to the brim with water, of which not a drop must be spilled.

The WATCHMAN [*From the height of the turret over the gate*] The torches of their vanguard can be seen at the corner of the Avenue of the East —— The sound of their artillery-wagons can be faintly heard ——

EMPRESS

Already at the corner of the Avenue of the East! —— Death is flying to us on wings [*She takes the cup full of poison which* CINNAMON *had hidden behind a stone*] The hour has come! —— [*To the* LADIES-IN-WAITING *around her, pointing to the pyre.*] As soon as the potion has accomplished its work, you will place me there, and when the flame mounts higher and clearer, then your service to your Empress will be terminated, you will empty the golden flask, to follow me. [*She puts down the cup of poison which she was about to raise to her lips.*] Faithful Prince, I wish to say good-bye to him —— Call him.

[*During the preceding dialogue, the* FAITHFUL

PRINCE, *at the back of the stage, a torch in his hand, superintends a group of* SOLDIERS, *who are using crowbars and pickaxes.*]

CINNAMON

Over yonder, is that not he?
[FAITHFUL PRINCE *orders the* SOLDIERS *to remove a rock, which hides a small bronze door.*]

EMPRESS

Ah, I knew ——

PEARL

What is he doing?

EMPRESS

What must be done! He too, realising that the hour has come for me to go to my last sleep, is preparing my couch. These galleries beneath the earth lead to my tomb.

[*The bronze door opens.* PEARL *kneels and hides her face.* GOLDEN LOTUS, *a little apart from the group, is kneeling near* ARROW-BEARER, *and speaks tenderly to him, as she smooths his forehead.*]

This proud tomb, long ago hewn out secretly, is of no use now. There rather, there in the beautiful flame and the eddying smoke, my spirit will ascend to the clouds —— Nothing of me shall remain for the hands of the Tartar to profane. In vain they will have surrounded me. I shall escape them, in the air ——

TRANQUIL BEAUTY [*Also kneeling*]

But Sovereign, since this tomb is secret and is inviolable, at least permit your attendants to bury you there, in magnificence. —— Permit that, oh, well beloved Sovereign;—— That flame, oh, why that flame? No, no, it is too horrible.

EMPRESS

Child, do you not know the history of our race? My ancestor, defeated in this same place, defeated as I am, killed himself —— An hour later his tomb was violated, his body was thrown into the street as food for the dogs and the vultures —— I have declared my will. Go call Faithful Prince. He wastes his strength in a vain task, when he is bleeding. See, the blood covers his robe. His wound has reopened, he pays no heed to it. At least let him spare time to bid me farewell —— Go, it is my wish. [TRANQUIL BEAUTY *rises and goes over to the* PRINCE. *During the preceding dialogue, he has been ordering the* SOLDIERS *to light more torches and to carry them into the vault.*]

TRANQUIL BEAUTY [*Advancing to* FAITHFUL PRINCE]

Prince! —— The Empress ——

[FAITHFUL PRINCE *approaches the* EMPRESS.]

SCENE VI.

The EMPRESS, FAITHFUL PRINCE, TRANQUIL BEAUTY, *The* CAPTAIN *of the* SOLDIERS, *A* WATCHMAN.

EMPRESS [*To* FAITHFUL PRINCE]

Prince, I wish to bid you farewell. My last spoken word must be to you, with my everlasting gratitude.

[*She raises the poison-cup to her lips.*]

FAITHFUL PRINCE   [*With a gesture as though to stop her.*]

No, my Divine Empress, no.   The hour of rest, alas! has not come for you or for me.   No, your hard task is not yet completed! ——

EMPRESS

My task, you say, is not yet completed?   But the palace is only a ruin.   The gates are giving way, the walls are crumbling —— This time we can withstand the attack only ten minutes —— it is the end! ——

FAITHFUL PRINCE

Alas, I know it all too well.   There is no hope.

EMPRESS

Then let me go —— the Tartars are returning. Listen, I too begin to hear their war-trumpets. You would not have that they should take your Empress alive, or even find her body to throw to the crows.

FAITHFUL PRINCE

Hear me, I entreat you! —— [*He motions to* VEILED-LIGHT, *who has just appeared at the back. The* EMPRESS *has set down the cup on a stone.*] We have deferred making known to you the last heroic service which we purpose to demand —— Permit your Councillor to convey to you our unanimous opinion.

VEILED-LIGHT [*Bending the knee*]

Oh, Majesty, 200,000 soldiers have died for you. The few hundred, also, who remain here within our walls, are about to sacrifice their lives at once. Do you wish them to die for a lost cause. [*He motions to the* CHIEF *of the* SOLDIERS *to approach.*] Deign to permit their chief to add his prayers to ours.

The CAPTAIN *of the* SOLDIERS, [*After bending the knee.*]

Proudly and without regret we give up our lives for our Sovereign —— May she too do what we have learned to expect of her marvellous courage, a thousand times greater than that of her humble defenders.

Veiled-Light

Oh, Majesty, we must envy these men who are about to die so gloriously. Our duty is otherwise; it is longer, it is more terrible.

Empress

Our duty longer and more terrible? —— Then what do you expect of me? Speak, what would you say. Your Empress will obey you, but speak at once, I do not understand. [*She takes again the golden cup.*]

Faithful Prince

What we must do, my beloved Sovereign, is to flee and live.

Empress [*Violently*]

Ah, no! All that you have demanded of me I have done, but I refuse to take flight like a coward.

Veiled-Light

To flee, alas! yes. But to escape from the enemy, to deprive them of the prize of war —— and thus their success will be but failure. Soon the blood of our heroes will inspire other heroes. A new army will rally to the cause of the Daughter of Heaven, and the war will begin again.

EMPRESS

And more blood will be spilt —— and the ravaged country will people the realm of the shades —— No, no, enough of death's —— I fear to have my reign handed down as that of a fatal and murderous Sovereign. All this blood! All this blood spilled for me! It seems to me that my very hands are red with it!

FAITHFUL PRINCE

The blood of your subjects is inexhaustible, and their devotion is limitless.

EMPRESS [*Suddenly becoming very calm and as though beseeching*]

But my courage is exhausted. [*Pointing to the* SOLDIERS, *who are piling wood upon the fire.*] I want to die with them.

FAITHFUL PRINCE

Live, that their death may not have been in vain. Live to bring back our young Emperor, whom the Army of the South is protecting for us. Live for us all and for him.

EMPRESS

My son! Oh, speak not that name. Do not, to influence me, do not try to touch upon that string, that alone I forbid you touch. At the very moment when you tore him from me, I had an intuition that I should never see him again, never again gaze upon his dear little face, his beautiful eyes —— I have courage to listen to all except when you speak to me of him,—— for then, do you not see, I become again a mother, nothing but a mother, like other women, and I have no longer, no longer the strength. —— [*She turns her head and begins to sob.*] Oh, not to belong to one's self, not even to be allowed to lay down on the roadside the burden of one's life! —— To be the impersonal idol of a whole people, to be dealt with in accordance with their will! To be a wretched fetish, whom all watch as carefully as the tablets of their ancestors on the family altar! ——

FAITHFUL PRINCE

You are the shining standard, the ever-radiant goddess, toward whom we turn in our supreme distress —— and you will do what millions of your subjects demand of you, through the mouths of these few brave men who are about to die.

THE WATCHMAN] *from the height of the turret,*] He hurls himself against their vanguard, the man who was here just now, the Messenger of peace —— with the three others who accompanied him. He hurls himself against their vanguard as though to make them halt. Yes, he wishes them to stop, that is it. And he seems to command like a master, and to inspire them with fear.

EMPRESS [*To the* WATCHMAN]
So! Let not that man's name be mentioned again to me. And you, poor Watchman, whose task is finished, you may come down and join your brothers in arms, to die with them. Of what concern to us now are the movements of the Tartars? We are no longer of this world. [*To* FAITHFUL PRINCE] But how, then, is what you asked of me possible? —— Surrounded on all sides, how and whither can we flee. Where can we hide? Where?

[*The* SOLDIERS, *having loosened the rock, are standing in front of the bronze door, still holding their crowbars and pickaxes. They have an air of expectancy.*]

FAITHFUL PRINCE
There in the tomb. On the cement lying all ready now to seal the rocks we shall throw dust —— as soon you shall have entered.——

The EMPRESS [*After a silence, speaking slowly, submissive and very melancholy*] In my grave entombed alive! Be it so! And after that?——

FAITHFUL PRINCE
There is a subterranean passage, which passes through the vaults where your father and your hus-

band sleep.   You know, as I do, that its end opens
out upon brushwood in the country, at the foot of
the Hill of Tortures.

EMPRESS

[*Quickly and breathlessly*]   If it is not already
obstructed by the soil, yes!   And all about the Hill
of Tortures the Tartars are encamped.

FAITHFUL PRINCE

We will wait until they are no longer there.

EMPRESS

And shall we have sufficient air in this vault,
where sleep our dead?

FAITHFUL PRINCE

Yes, I believe so —— but let us take this potion
with us which you wished to drink a while ago.

EMPRESS   [*Very excitedly*]

And if the Tartars take us there, if they track us
like beasts of the night, hunted into their burrows?
Remember how they violated the tomb of my ancestor.

FAITHFUL PRINCE

It was not secret, like yours.

EMPRESS   [*Still in great excitement*]

And, clothes wherewith to escape through the

country where the enemy roams at large? [*Pointing to her uniform.*] Not these, for sure?

FAITHFUL PRINCE

Some taken from the enemy will serve admirably —— The ground must be covered with them.

EMPRESS

Rags torn from some festering corpse, is it thus you would clothe your Empress! —— So be it, even to that I consent —— But how can we live in the depths of that tomb? Since we are not yet of the Shades, we must eat, you know that. I divided my last grains of rice this morning with you and my soldiers! —— What then?

FAITHFUL PRINCE   [*Pointing to the tomb.*]

The consecrated cakes there on the table of the dead.

EMPRESS

Horror and sacrilege!

VEILED-LIGHT

There is no sacrilege, when the safety of the Bright Dynasty is at stake. The August Shades will come in person to invite us to eat. Our sacrifice will make them indulgent and favourable.

EMPRESS   [*Slowly*]

And so I must be the one to live in the chill gloom with no certainty of ever coming forth.   I must be the one to creep about like a ghost in the vaults peopled by phantoms, groping my hands over the pious offerings shrivelling on the altars of the dead —— Aye, it is indeed more terrible than dying here. But I accept it.   Lead me on, I am resigned.

The WATCHMAN   [*From the top of the wall*]

The Tartars have stopped their march, a small group is running toward us, unarmed, but carrying signs on long poles.   In spite of the darkness, it looks like a message which grants pardon.

EMPRESS

Ha, a forced pardon —— that would be more insulting still.   Bury me in my tomb, Prince, before they come.

FAITHFUL PRINCE   [*Pointing to* VEILED-LIGHT]

Your Councillor and I will follow you into the tomb, and perhaps two of these young girls if they feel brave enough for the ordeal.

SCENE VII.

The same, the LADIES-IN-WAITING.

EMPRESS

So here are my household, my court of death, and
doubtless my last retinue of mourners; just four
persons! [*To the* LADIES-IN-WAITING] Which
two of you, my maidens, will have the courage to
follow me down those gloomy paths below?

LADIES-IN-WAITING   [*Bowing*]

All of us, we are all ready. Your Majesty has
but to deign to name two of us.

EMPRESS   [*After a pause*]

Tranquil Beauty, Cinnamon!
[TRANQUIL BEAUTY *and* CINNAMON *approach
the* EMPRESS.]

All of you are dear to me, but I have called those
who in adversity have shown the bravest hearts.
[*To the others.*]   And you, my sweet flowers, so
untimely faded, may the Water of the Great Deliverance convey you easily beyond this world
through the peace of sleep.

PEARL

We have given it all to the wounded.

ANOTHER LADY

Our flasks are empty.

PEARL

The flames terrify us —— but we know how to
die, noble Sovereign.

ANOTHER LADY

The Lake in the garden is deep, around the Isle of
Jade.

PEARL

As soon as we have conducted your Majesty to
the threshold of the tomb we shall repair to the lake-
side.

ANOTHER LADY

Deep in the mud, where we shall sleep tranquilly,
The Lotus will entwine us in her roots and we shall
live again in her flowers.

EMPRESS

[*To* GOLDEN LOTUS, *who is seated to the left,
holding in her lap the dying* ARROW-BEARER'S
head.]   And you, Golden Lotus?

GOLDEN LOTUS

Oh, Majesty, receive from here my last greeting
—— To leave him, to set down his head, forgive
me if I have not the courage ——

[*The trumpets and gongs of the* TARTARS *are*

*heard without, with a shouting which grows nearer
and nearer.*]

EMPRESS [*To* ARROW-BEARER *and* GOLDEN
LOTUS]

Alas, poor lovers without a to-morrow, here is
the marriage gift from your Empress. [*She pours
out some poison into her golden cup and gives it to
them.*] Farewell, may you be united in the clouds.
[*To* FAITHFUL PRINCE] Let us go, Prince, show
me the way. I am ready.

The CHIEF *of the* SOLDIERS [*advancing to* FAITH-
FUL PRINCE.]

Prince, speak for us.

FAITHFUL PRINCE

Your Majesty, your soldiers ask one more favour of you.

EMPRESS

Is it then in my power still to do aught for them?
All, all that they ask I will give.

FAITHFUL PRINCE

You desired to know why they were piling so
much wood on the fire. It was for themselves.
They want to die before the entrance of the Tartars,
and this is the last request that they make, that you
will set the torch to their funeral pile.

[*The* CHIEF *of the* SOLDIERS *kneels, and hands a lighted torch to the* EMPRESS.]

EMPRESS [*Taking the torch and addressing the* SOLDIERS.] My well beloved soldiers, be assured that your Empress will soon follow you into the land of the Shades. She accepts your request that she should flee, only that she may try to avenge you. But if happier days smile upon the Bright Dynasty she will refuse to live them. Before you all, she takes this solemn vow; When once her relentless task is at an end, she will hasten to join you in the land of the Shades —— Oh, victims that are more than men, oh, conquered ones that wear the halo of glory! Oh, my heroic army! —— A day shall come when the story of your sublime death shall be engraved in letters of gold on the Imperial Jade, that posterity may weep for you. [*She sets the torch to the pile*] and that the brightness of your funeral pile may dazzle the world for ever! ——

[*The pile takes fire. The* SOLDIERS *throw themselves into the flame as they sing.*]

The SOLDIERS

Long live our King! Long and happy life to our King!
[*A cloud of black smoke envelopes them. The sound of an approaching gong is heard at reg-*

ular intervals, and then the voice of a TARTAR HER-
ALD.]

THE TARTAR HERALD [*outside, in the distance.*] The Command of the Emperor! Tremble
and obey!

FAITHFUL PRINCE [*Hastily to the* CAPTAIN *of
the soldiers.*] Let the rock be replaced as I told
you. Block it up quick and throw earth upon the
cement, and a pile of dust. [*The* CAPTAIN *rejoins
the few men who are standing before the tomb, still
holding their crowbars and pickaxes. The* EM-
PRESS, FAITHFUL PRINCE, VEILED-LIGHT, TRAN-
QUIL BEAUTY, *and* CINNAMON *go towards the
bronze door. The other* LADIES-IN-WAITING *follow, and kneel as they approach the door.*]

EMPRESS [*At the threshold of the tomb, addressing the four who are to enter with her.*] Go
in before me. I will be the last to pass through.
My funeral is this! —— And then I wish to gaze
for the last time upon my heroes and my beautiful
palace yonder, still standing out in relief. [*To the
kneeling* LADIES] Arise, my cherished maidens.
Do not delay. The lake to which you go is not
near by.

[*The* LADIES-IN-WAITING *go out, hand-in-hand,
and as they disappear their sobs are heard. The*
EMPRESS *sets foot on the threshold of the door and
then turns round like one inspired, watching the*

flames of the pyre, which rises higher and higher.
She raises her arms as though in an ecstasy.]

EMPRESS

See the glorious red flame! See the beautiful
eddying smoke. It is bright within my palace for
the last time. And I see them too, those noble
souls, mounting ever higher and higher in the dark
whirling spirals of smoke!

SOLDIERS   [*Singing in the flames*]

Ten thousand years! Ten thousand years.

EMPRESS   [*To the* SOLDIERS]

Go, my brave men!—— Soar up on high, fly
to the heaven of your ancestors, ascend to the god
of the clouds.

SOLDIERS   [*More feebly*]

Ten thousand years, ten thousand years!

[*The* TARTAR's *gong is heard ever closer and
closer.*]

EMPRESS   [*To the* SOLDIERS]

I too am doomed like you, be sure of that! Only
a little later my soul will take flight. But already
I am dead, dead to all save vengeance, save the fury
of battle, save merciless hate. And now I must
shut my door of bronze. [*To the* SOLDIERS *who
hold the crowbars.*] Cement it well, my friends,
to hide your Empress! Replace the heavy boulder.

Immure this living corpse in her tomb. [*She closes the bronze door after her. The* CAPTAIN *and the few men who remain replace the rock, hastily piling cement and dust upon it.*]

The Voice of the TARTAR HERALD [*now at the foot of the wall*] The command of the Emperor! Tremble and obey! To all without condition, pardon and liberty! Open your gates and have no fear, the Emperor grants pardon to all.

One of the SOLDIERS [*who is cementing the rock*] The insult of your pardon comes too late. Before you can break down our walls, we shall all be dead.

Voice of TARTAR HERALD

Open and have no fear, our Emperor grants life to all.

ANOTHER SOLDIER

Nay, there shall not even be dead to receive your pardon, nought but ashes!

CAPTAIN *of* SOLDIERS [*as he finishes cementing the rock against the door of the Imperial tomb*] Our beautiful Phœnix, for want of power to spread her wings, has vanished under the earth.

The voices of the SOLDIERS [*becoming feebler*

in the flames and smoke]   Ten thousand years to
the Bright Dynasty!   Ten thousand years!
   [*The flames and smoke envelope the entire scene.*]

CURTAIN

ACT FOUR.

First Tableau.

[*Before the curtain rises the shouts of the crowd are heard, mingled with sound of gongs and bells. The execution-ground under the ramparts of Peking. A colossal grey wall with battlements, occupies the back of the stage, and, on the left, disappears from view in the distance. Chinese prisoners are attached to stakes all along the wall, others are in the cangue, under a huge red signboard. Here and there decapitated heads hang dripping from spikes. There are blood-stains all over the ground. A noisy crowd hurries along the front of the scene. The men wearing modern Peking costume, long queues, blue cotton robes and goat-skin tunics. The* TARTAR *women, of lower-class, wear a horn-like coiffure with large artificial flowers in it. In the foreground, to the left, is the large tent of the* TARTAR GENERAL; *of greenish leather, with a yellow roofing, surmounted by a silver bell-turret. It is wide open. The interior is carpeted with the skins of wild beasts; a circular table surrounds the central pole; carpets, camp-stools, a little table, and a square banner bearing the name of the* GENERAL. GUARDS *and* SOLDIERS, *with naked sabres. Camels are lying all around, among bales of goods and arms. Carriages, palanquins.*]

*As the curtain rises, the crowd continues to shout
wildly. Vendors of hot drinks are walking
about with copper urns on their backs; barbers
are ringing their bells; blind conjurers are
playing the flute, sweetmeat-pedlars are striking gongs. The executioners in the immediate
foreground are wiping the dripping blades of
their swords.]*

SCENE I.

The EXECUTIONERS, *the* CROWD.

FIRST EXECUTIONER [*As he wipes his sword,
speaking to two young women standing near him*]
Our arms are pretty tired, my little beauties.

ONE WOMAN

Ah! But your arms look very strong, Master
Executioner.

THE EXECUTIONER

Strong, well I don't say they are not.   But all the
same ——

A FLOWER-PEDLAR

Imperial peonies, lotus of all kinds, every flower
of the season.

A FRUIT PEDLAR

Sweet as honey, red fruit of the mountains.
A TARTAR CHILD [*Approaching the* EXECU-

TIONER.] Mr. Executioner, do you have to strike very hard to cut off their heads?

[*Some men carrying a bucket full of water suspended on their shoulders, begin to swill the ground with a large wooden ladle.*]

EXECUTIONER

It requires skill, my little lamb —— to find just the right place —— skill and force too, of course —— Ah! I can tell you, our business is not learnt in a day ——

A SWEETMEAT-PEDLAR

[*Ringing a small bell*] They have the flavour of sugar-cane, the sweets that I have for sale.

FRUIT-VENDOR

Ay, ay! White as tallow, white as jade, my fresh melons.

TWO BEGGARS [*Playing guitars*]

Come listen to the legend of the King of the Dragons.

[*They sing in a very shrill voice.*]
 Near the Bamboo Lake,
  Three owls, three owls.

SECOND EXECUTIONER

[*To some other women as he points to the prisoners tied to stakes.*] What, the second group there? Their turn will come very soon. The

Chief Executioner has given us a few minutes' rest, and we've earned it well, haven't we? [*He hails a pedlar of drinks and orders one for himself.*]

HABERDASHER [*Striking a small bell*]

All the latest styles in my stock!—— Look, young women, look, young girls!

ONE TARTAR WOMAN [*To Another*]

Oh, I'm not one of those who take pleasure in seeing heads cut off —— and, besides, the sight is always the same. No, it is their goddess whom I wish to see.

SECOND TARTAR WOMAN

Their goddess?—— their Empress?—— Ah, and so do I. All of us want to see their goddess. She is the one who interests us the most.

THIRD TARTAR WOMAN

And do you suppose they will show her to you?

SECOND WOMAN

Why not? They are showing us all their generals and princes, and all the rest of them —— Prisoners are made to be seen, that is why they were brought here to Peking.

THIRD WOMAN

Oh, yes, but she —— it seems that while she was being brought here, she was treated with every consideration that could be shown to a queen. And the Emperor has had her placed in the Forbidden City, you know; in his very Palace indeed.

Second Woman

It is said that her eyes are so wonderful that ordinary people like us cannot meet their gaze.

Jasmine-Flower

Yes, and I should be afraid to look at her! A woman who has been dead — for she was dead for at least two moons, you know!

Second Woman

Jasmine Flower believes everything that is told her.

Jasmine

Why, every one knows that she was dead —— For two moons, I tell you! She spent two moons in her grave.

Fruit-Vendor

Ay, ay, white as tallow, white as jade, new melon!

First Woman

It is well known that bullets and grapeshot passed through her as through a ghost. [*Seeing a* Captain *of the* Soldiers, *who is standing near.*] There, ask Lee-Phuang, who was there when she was taken. Isn't it true, Lee-Phuang?

LEE-PHUANG

Oh, yes, I was a witness myself. The bullets could not touch this goddess of theirs!

Two subordinate OFFICERS *[leading to the execution-ground a new group of Chinese prisoners, with hands tied behind them, among whom bringing up the rear, is the* FAITHFUL PRINCE, *his garments all stained and torn.]*

Make room, make room!

[The prisoners pass along to join the others who are awaiting their turn to be beheaded at the foot of the wall.]

LEE-PHUANG. *[To the* WOMEN *who questioned him]* You see the last one in the line, look at him, the one who walks with so haughty an air? He is the greatest chief of the Nanking rebels. His name is the Faithful Prince, he was the right hand of the Goddess in battle, he was always at her side.

HABERDASHER   *[Striking his bell]*

All the latest styles in my stock! Look young women, have a look, young girls!

SCENE II.

FAITHFUL PRINCE.   *The* TARTAR GENERAL
The TARTAR GENERAL   *[coming out of his tent and*

saluting FAITHFUL PRINCE, *who brings up the rear of the last group of condemned men.*]

Enter here, noble captive. Look not over yonder. Each man should die but once, and you would die each time you saw a head fall. Is it not punishment enough for you to be the last of all the victims?

FAITHFUL PRINCE

Perhaps my presence may strengthen my poor soldiers, so simple in their heroism.

TARTAR GENERAL

No, no, your suffering only adds to their pain —— Grant a loyal enemy the great honour of passing the last minutes of your glorious life in his tent. You are now above wordly trivialities and implacable hates.

FAITHFUL PRINCE

The sword is not responsible, not even the executioner.

TARTAR GENERAL

Nor yet even the General!
[*The new prisoners are tied to the stake.*]

FAITHFUL PRINCE

I bear no malice.
[*He enters the tent with the* TARTAR GENERAL.]

TARTAR GENERAL

And I make no boast. I know that the sages disapprove of war and hold that the work of the conqueror amounts to no more than the dust of ten thousand skeletons ——

FAITHFUL PRINCE

And that those who triumph deserve no more than the honour of a funeral.

TARTAR GENERAL

Yes, the glory of arms is indeed but the smoke of a fire! [*They seat themselves on camp-stools, and rice wine is served to them. Throughout the following dialogue executions are in progress in the foreground, amid the shouts of the crowd. Every minute the sword of an executioner describes a circle in the air, and as each head falls, it is hung up on the great wall of Peking. Deafening shrieks and cries accompany the conversation of the two men in the tent.*]

TARTAR GENERAL

Before passing from this world, have you not some mission for your dear ones which you might desire carried out? I would undertake it respectfully.

Faithful Prince

Beyond a doubt all who were dear to me have perished. I thank you for your considerate offer.

Tartar General

Have you no last desire?

Faithful Prince

One only. To know the fate of our Empress. She was fighting too in that dreadful battle where I was taken prisoner. Is she alive or dead, free or captive?

Tartar General

She is living, a captive only a fortnight since, and yesterday was brought to Peking, not far from here in the Forbidden City.

Faithful Prince

She is not far from here, my Sovereign! Ah, if only the gods, wearied with afflicting us, would permit —— To know that she is so near! ——

Tartar General

At the end of that battle which was so great an honour to the defeated, she succeeded in escaping with a thousand soldiers. But her retreat was cut off, and the Warrior Empress would have been captured lŏng before had not contradictory orders, hindering our movements, enabled her to delay her capture from day to day. You would have thought someone in great authority was watching over her with wonderful solicitude, warning her of dangers or endeavouring to turn them aside from her.

FAITHFUL PRINCE

May he live long happy days, and may his fame be imperishable!

TARTAR GENERAL

Oh, when will this dreadful war cease, which is renewed and has already soaked the soil of our country in the blood of her sons?

FAITHFUL PRINCE

I fear it will never end until one of the two races has been exterminated —— Yet perhaps the hatred would be less intense if the conquerors after their victory would treat the defeated with more clemency. Let there not be so many executions, so much bloodshed. Each soldier who can no longer defend his life should be sacred.

TARTAR GENERAL

Pardon was offered to your soldiers if they would yield. All refused.

FAITHFUL PRINCE

Their heroism should be only an additional reason for sparing them.

TARTAR GENERAL

What can be done? Our duty is to obey.

FAITHFUL PRINCE

Not to the extent of a crime. A little stone can ofttimes retard the course of a heavy chariot. We, the chieftains, by sacrificing only our own lives could thereby save the crowds.

TARTAR GENERAL

How could that be?

FAITHFUL PRINCE

By opposing unrighteousness. Do you remember? There was once another war similar in every way to this. The city was sacked, the command was given to the executioners to cut off all heads as now. But a young officer, maddened by grief at the thought of such carnage, found words wherewith to beseech the general to be merciful, or at least to restrict the number of executions, with the result that he consented to limit the massacre to the length of time which is required to burn a stick of incense. The incense was lighted and the first head was about to fall, when the young officer trembling

with horror seized the stick, reduced it to powder
and ran to the executioner, crying aloud " It is finished, it is finished. Pardon has been declared."
Then, since he had disobeyed, he immediately
dashed his head against a rock. The people erected
a temple in memory of this hero, which is still to be
seen on a high hill and whose steps have for many
centuries been constantly covered with fresh flowers.

TARTAR GENERAL   [*Pensively*]
In memory of this hero the people erected a
temple! ——

SCENE III.

The same, the CROWD, *then an* OFFICER.
[*For the last few minutes the* CROWD *has been
protesting more violently against the slaughter.
As a new group of prisoners is brought to the
place, the protest becomes more insistent.*]

THE CROWD
Enough! enough!

A VOICE
The Ministers of the Empire are a set of butchers!
A MAN   [*Raising himself on the shoulders of
his neighbours*]   Enough, enough! Death to the
tigers!

FAITHFUL PRINCE   [*In the tent, seeing the* TAR-
TAR GENERAL *rise.*]   No doubt my time has come.

TARTAR GENERAL

No! No! Remain where you are, we shall be
told.

ANOTHER MAN

Yes, death to the tigers!
[*He leans over and dips the end of his girdle into
the blood*]   I am going to write it on this wall.
Death to the tigers!
[*He gets up on a stone, and begins to trace some
characters with the end of his girdle. The* GEN-
ERAL *comes out of the tent.*]

AN OFFICER

Some men here at once! —— Disperse this in-
solent crowd! —— Arrest the man who is writing.

TARTAR GENERAL   [*Advancing quickly*]
Who dares to give orders without my consent?

THE OFFICER

My lord, when a riot is beginning, is it not my
duty?

TARTAR GENERAL

You have no other duty than to obey. [*With
a gesture he dismisses the* SOLDIERS, *who have ad-
vanced to seize the man.*] The executioners must

be tired.   Let their chief give them leave to rest again.

OFFICER

For how many minutes?

TARTAR GENERAL

As long as my sword shall remain fixed here.
[*He plunges his sword into the ground.*]

FAITHFUL PRINCE

[*In a whisper to the* GENERAL.]   Take care, my generous enemy.   Perhaps it may be thought that you are afraid.

TARTAR GENERAL

Of the living, no! —— But of spectres, yes, it is true; I am afraid of spectres.
[*They enter the tent together. The crowd, whose excitement is increasing, moves away from the execution-ground, thereby giving a full view of the headless bodies which are lying on the ground, and of the pools of blood. The street-sellers recommence their cries and their music.*]

FLOWER-VENDOR

Royal peonies, lotus of all kinds, every flower of the season.

TARTAR GENERAL   [*In his tent, to* FAITHFUL PRINCE]

You see, I am compromising myself like the hero of your legend, and yet no temple will be raised in my honour.

FAITHFUL PRINCE

But you do not hope to save those of my men who are still alive?

GENERAL

Who knows, as long as their heads are on their shoulders?—— You heard the noise outside? —— The angry crowd grew greater and greater. A short riot has often delivered many victims. I may be compelled to yield. Heaven grant it!

FAITHFUL PRINCE

Your noble generosity encourages me to ask a favour of you.

TARTAR GENERAL

It will be a great joy to me to grant it.

FAITHFUL PRINCE

Before taking my place against that bloody wall, I would greatly desire to have one hour's freedom, on my word of honour ——

TARTAR GENERAL

The word of a man such as you are is stronger

than a chain of iron on his feet, or a canque of
cedar wood about his shoulders —— an hour, yes!
Even an hour and a half, we can wait —— The
use which you wish to make of it perhaps I can
imagine. You dream of seeing again your adored
Empress —— There, alas! I am unable to aid
you. May the gods come to your assistance! ——
[*Offering him a robe embroidered in gold, which
is hanging from the tent-pole.*] One thing alone I
can do for you. Consent to wear one of my robes.
It will be a safeguard for you.

FAITHFUL PRINCE
How could I dare?

TARTAR GENERAL
I beseech you —— This garment will be to me
the more precious because it has protected you
[*He passes the robe to* FAITHFUL PRINCE, *who
no longer protests, then he raises a curtain at the
back to the tent.*] Go that way, Prince! ——

[FAITHFUL PRINCE *goes out.*]

SCENE IV.

The GENERAL, *A* COURIER *from the* EMPEROR,
An OFFICER, *The* PRISONERS, *The* CROWD.

[*There is a great stir in the crowd, which is shouting wildly. In the distance trumpets are heard. The* TARTAR GENERAL, *coming out of his tent, speaks to an* OFFICER.]

TARTAR GENERAL
What is that? The ceremonial salute. What is happening now?

The OFFICER
A courier from the Emperor. [*The* SOLDIERS *stand in file on either side and bend the knee. The* COURIER *is on horseback, and is carrying over his shoulder a small packet, wrapped in yellow silk.*]

COURIER   [*As he dismounts*]
An order from the Emperor! [*Two* SOLDIERS *place a table on which the letter is deposited, then the incense-sticks are lighted. The* TARTAR GENERAL *quickly dons his ceremonial robe, salutes the message three times, and at last takes it.*]

TARTAR GENERAL   [*To the* COURIER, *after he has examined the envelope*] Why does that order arrive so late? It was sent at daybreak from the Forbidden City, and the distance is not long.

COURIER
That is true, my lord. But ill-intentioned men were posted at several places along my route. I

had to take a roundabout course, and my horse knocked over many people before surmounting the obstacles.

TARTAR GENERAL   [*In a low voice*]

May Heaven deliver our Emperor from the evil ones who oppose his will!

COURIER   [*also speaking low*]

May Heaven hear your prayer, for the well-being of the people!

TARTAR GENERAL   [*Opens the letter. In an aside after having read it*]   This saves many lives, without counting my own —— [*To the* CROWD.] Order of the Emperor. All listen! " This is my express will. I grant unconditional pardon to all the captives of war, chiefs and soldiers, and give them their entire liberty. Respect this."

[*He shows the Imperial seal.*]

THE CROWD

Ten thousand years, ten thousand years to our Emperor.

[*The* SOLDIERS *at once set the prisoners free.*]

TARTAR GENERAL   [*To the* CROWD]

Listen again. This order should have arrived in time to save all the condemned. The obstacles set in the path of the messenger are the cause of a misfortune which cannot be repaired. Our master was disobeyed and is not responsible.

CROWD

Curse upon the unfaithful ministers! Death to the tigers!

[*The women also hasten to unchain the prisoners, who draw near the* GENERAL.]

ONE OFFICER   [*In a whisper to another*]

What seditious cries our General permits!

SECOND OFFICER

Say rather he encourages them.

TARTAR GENERAL   [*To the* PRISONERS]

My friends, listen to wise advice. Do not remain long in this accursed place. All around the mighty Dragon who has freed you, wild beasts are shrieking, exasperated because they have lost their prey —— Go at once, do not lose a moment. But do not escape by way of the country, you would be too easily found. Disperse and wander through the great city. In the Chinese Quarter the crowd will not betray you.

PRISONERS

We will follow your advice. May Heaven bestow its choicest blessings upon you!

[*They bow and disperse. The* GENERAL *takes his sword, which he had stuck into the ground and slowly replaces it in its scabbard.*]

THE CROWD
Death to the tigers!   Ten thousand years to our Emperor!
[*As the curtain is lowered the shouts of* PEDLARS *are heard.*]

THE FLOWER-SELLER
Royal peonies, Lotus of all kinds, every flower of the season!

HABERDASHER
All the latest styles in my stock!   Look, young women; have a look, young girls!

Second Tableau

[*The great throne-room in the palace at Peking,
entirely decorated in red and gold. The throne is
in the middle of a dais, to which lead three staircases flanked by incense-burners and emblems. Pil-
lars of red laquer support a lofty ceiling, on which
are enormous writhing dragons among red clouds;
the largest standing out so clearly that it looks ready
to fall from heaven, holds in its jaws a golden orb,
just above the throne. The floor is covered by a
yellow carpet, with dragons more than fifty feet in
length woven into the design. On one side of the
stage is a marble chime, suspended by golden chains
from a huge frame work, whose feet are of gold
and represent monsters and whose upper angles are
ornamented with golden phœnixes spreading their
wings toward the ceiling. Near the principal entrance two* EUNUCHS *are holding dust-dispellers of
rhinoceros-hide. Preparations are being made for
a solemn audience, to commemorate the triumph of
the* TARTAR ARMY. *Large blocks of porcelain,
representing monsters, are arranged in line on the
carpet. They mark the places where the various
bodies of dignitaries are to stand and to prostrate
themselves. Persons in gala robes come and go*

*hurriedly. They are speaking in whispers, and
walk noiselessly, in respectful attitudes. They bow
as they pass the throne.*]

SCENE I.

Palace, OFFICIALS, DIGNITARIES, *and* MASTERS
of the CEREMONIES.

FIRST MASTER OF CEREMONIES
[*Placing in line one of the last blocks of porcelain*] There, the eighteenth group of high liter-
ates will stand there, facing the throne, but somewhat obliquely.

SECOND MASTER OF CEREMONIES
Everything seems to me in perfect order. We
shall soon be ready.

AN OFFICIAL
So they say, indeed. He has been downcast and
melancholy for several days, it seems as though
each fresh victory of his army affected him like a
disaster.

THIRD OFFICER
Yes, no one would have supposed that he would
demand so elaborate a ceremony to celebrate his
triumph.

FOURTH OFFICER

And have you heard the news? The prisoner is to make her appearance here.

THIRD OFFICER

Who?

FOURTH OFFICER

Who? How can you ask? The great, the only one. She of whom everyone speaks — the Ex-Empress of the rebels.

FIFTH OFFICER

Ah, the goddess! So now we are going to see her.

SIXTH OFFICER

And we can judge of her supernatural power —— unless she has lost it.

FOURTH OFFICER

Oh, power she still has. Yesterday evening, by order of the Emperor, two eunuchs were decapitated simply for having announced to her the death of her son without preliminary forms.

THIRD OFFICER

And I know something, too, from the Governess of the Palace —— To-day the goddess deigned to speak, to request mourning garments —— So they searched the wardrobes of the late Empress

Regent for all that was most magnificent in the way of white robes and shoes!

SCENE II.

The same.   The GRAND CHAMBERLAIN

GRAND CHAMBERLAIN   [*Entering by a door at back*]

An order from the Emperor!   [*All listen with bowed heads.*]   Let the members of the Privy Council, Ministers, and Dignitaries, robed in their costumes of state, meet in silence in the galleries near the throne-room, ready to enter when his Majesty strikes this gong three times.   [*He points to the large gong at the foot of the steps of the throne.*]   Let no one be here, and guards at all the doors!

[*All bow and prepare to go out.*]

SCENE III.

The Same, A HERALD, *and the* GRAND MASTER *of* CEREMONIES.

The HERALD   [*Appearing at the door and holding in his hand a large lacquer signboard mounted on a golden handle.*]   Silence!

The GRAND MASTER.   [*Entering with* FOUNT-IN-
THE-FOREST]

Let all depart! Close the doors. Here comes
the Emperor.

[*All skurry out except the* GRAND MASTER *and*
FOUNT-IN-THE-FOREST, *who prostrate themselves
as the* EMPEROR *appears.*]

SCENE IV.

The EMPEROR, FOUNT., *the* GRAND MASTER *of*
CEREMONIES.

EMPEROR   [*In full regalia, his expression som-
bre*]

How many heads did you say had already fallen?

GRAND MASTER

Barely fifty, sire.   Your General, as though with
a presentiment of the clemency of your Majesty, had
proceeded with audacious lack of energy.

EMPEROR

He shall be rewarded by Heaven and by me.   As
for the grandees of my court who dared to stop my
Courier, have them found at once and dealt with
by the executioner to-morrow.   Why do the gods
permit that in my lofty position, happiness should

be almost unrealisable, when murder is so easy?
Now go! [*Indicating* FOUNT-IN-THE-FOREST]   I
wish to speak with my councillor.

[*The* GRAND MASTER *goes out.*]

SCENE V.

EMPEROR, FOUNT.

EMPEROR   [*To* FOUNT, *who is still prostrate*]
Arise, friend, we are alone.   You have already
guessed my project, have you not?   I want her to
come here, near me.   [*Pointing to the throne.*]
Pale and in the white of her deep mourning as she
is, I want her to come here, to sit beside me on my
throne —— To-day, I am going to present her to
my people as my affianced bride.   Let the Dignitaries of my Court prostrate themselves before their
Empress, at the same time as before their Emperor
—— without her there is neither Empire nor
triumph for me ——

FOUNT

She has consented?

EMPEROR

Alas, I do not know if she will agree.   I have
postponed till now that meeting so full at once of

charm and terror. It is to-day and here that we shall see each other again for the first time —— May Heaven help me! You will say that I am still a child; I wished to invest our supreme moment with all magnificence. Ah, if only there were not between us the death of her son, I should tremble less.

FOUNT

But you did all in your power to save him. Since your conscience cannot reproach you, sire, it is better for your plans that the child should be resting in peace among the shades. To impose him upon your Tartars would have been dangerous indeed —— Whereas now, the two Dynasties may blend, another son be born, of your blood and hers.

EMPEROR

A son born to me by her! Oh, friend, be silent. The dreams that are too beautiful, one must not speak of. [*He strikes the gong lightly.*] But come, the dreaded moment of seeing her again has arrived. Come! [*To an* OFFICIAL *who enters in response to the gong.*] Let the prisoner be brought here, with all the respect which I have commanded. Go! [*Recalling the* OFFICIAL *as he is leaving.*] Wait a moment! [*To* FOUNT, *who is going too.*] No, her pride would be offended at being ushered into my presence. Rather, let her be the first to arrive, and I will follow, appearing before her with

the air of one vanquished, begging pardon.   [*To
the waiting* OFFICIAL.]   As soon as I leave, bring
the Empress here and leave her alone.   Now you
may go!

[*Exit the* OFFICIAL *at the back.*]

FOUNT [*as he goes out with the* EMPRESS]

She loves you, sire.   Have confidence.   Who is
the woman, even though she be almost a goddess,
who would not yield?

EMPEROR

She!   Only she!——

FOUNT

But, as she loved you once——

EMPEROR

And to-day must she not hate me?   How much
blood has been spilt by traitors despite my command!   How has my decree of pardon been inter-
cepted or changed to a death warrant!——
The hate, the implacable hate of our two peoples
ever triumphs.

FOUNT

But how many lives you have saved!——   And
she must too know that.

EMPEROR [*as he goes out*]

Oh, that hour whose memory still enchants my

heart! That hour there, in the garden of her palace, in the midst of that crowd where we were so alone, when she gazed upon me, when our souls were united in one supreme rapture —— But now at the thought of seeing her again, I tremble like a guilty man.

[*Exit the* EMPEROR, *with his councillor, through a side door. Two eunuchs and two women attendants conduct the* EMPRESS *to the foot of the throne, and after having prostrated themselves retire, leaving her alone. She is in white robes of mourning, her hands are tied by a silken cord.*]

SCENE VI

The EMPRESS, *then* FAITHFUL PRINCE

EMPRESS [*Soliloquising*]
Such consideration has been shown me that I am terrified, more terrified than at torture and death. Why am I in his palace, instead of in a prison? —— What can he, what dares he hope? What does he desire of me?

FAITHFUL PRINCE
[*In the dress of the* TARTAR GENERAL, *running into the room and prostrating himself at the feet of the* EMPRESS] Oh! Heaven is merciful to grant

me the opportunity once again before my death to prostrate myself at the feet of my adored Empress.

EMPRESS [*Calm but bewildered*]

You? You here? —— Dear Prince —— Have we then departed this life? Is this our reunion beyond the grave? If not, whence have you come, how, by what witchcraft have you passed these dreadful walls?

FAITHFUL PRINCE [*Still prostrated*]

Boldness does not count the cost, when there is no longer anything to lose —— And, beyond all doubt, the gods were with me —— Yes, I entered as if by witchcraft as you say, I passed the walls and the guarded gates —— One of his soldiers acted as my guide —— I gave him all the gold I had left. Forgive me, I am weeping, I know not whether for joy or grief. For joy it must be — since my only wish was for this one privilege — to see Your Majesty for the last time, to tell her on my knees of my passionate adoration —— which at the gates of death cannot be an offence —— and above all to offer her the wondrous gift, which will deliver her from the conqueror's worst outrages. My mission as faithful subject is now concluded by this last service, by the glorious present which I have brought to my Empress.

EMPRESS

Poison! [*With a triumphant cry of deliverance.*] Ah!——

FAITHFUL PRINCE [*Offering her a dagger*]

Poison, alas! I was unable to bring. This is the best I can offer.

EMPRESS

Ah, well, that will answer the purpose. Kill me before He comes!

FAITHFUL PRINCE [*Rising and drawing back in horror*]

My well beloved sovereign!—— Ask not that of your faithful servant, who has always obeyed you. Do not command him to do what is beyond his strength.

EMPRESS

You will not?—— Then give it to me! I will strike myself. I will make the attempt. I shall succeed.

FAITHFUL PRINCE [*Noticing that her hands are tied*]

But your hands—— To think that I had not seen!

EMPRESS

Ah! That is true.

FAITHFUL PRINCE

May I untie them?   Have we time?

EMPRESS

No, it will take too long.   Hide the weapon in the fold of my gown.

[*The* PRINCE *still hesitates.*]

You do not dare?   It is forbidden to touch your Sovereign!   Nay, but you may do so, your Empress now is as one already dead.

FAITHFUL PRINCE [*Hiding weapon in her gown*]

But how will you be able to use it?

EMPRESS

He will have them unbound, he before whom I shall soon appear.   And then is not one permitted to change one's mind so near to death?   I desired you to kill me before he came.   Now I prefer to see him again, the Emperor.

FAITHFUL PRINCE

To see him again?   You know then who he is?

EMPRESS

Yes.   Stay with me until he comes.

FAITHFUL PRINCE

Oh, no!   I must not be found here.

EMPRESS

What matters it now, at the point we have reached?

FAITHFUL PRINCE

Because — over yonder — the last heads are falling. They are calling for those that remain. It is time — my turn is coming. They gave me one hour's liberty on my word of honour. I do not want it to be thought that I have fled.

EMPRESS

Ah, yes! Then go, Prince. Farewell! I shall soon join you — you and all my faithful ones. Tell those who are about to die that I shall be with them soon ——

[FAITHFUL PRINCE *hurries out.*]

SCENE VII

The EMPEROR.   *The* EMPRESS

[*The* EMPEROR *enters and approaches her. The* EMPRESS, *her eyes lowered, stands motionless.*]

EMPEROR

Daughter of Heaven, deign to raise your eyes to gaze upon the heart-broken conqueror who bows before you. Deign to look and to recognise him.

Doubtless you will remember him. But can you
feel anything save utter hatred for him?

EMPRESS

[*Far away, her eyes still lowered.*] To recognise him, I do not need to hear his voice again nor
to gaze upon his face. The light has dawned upon
my mind during the hours of my captivity. Before
I was brought in here, I knew full well into whose
presence I was coming.

[*A silence, during which the* EMPEROR *remains
bowed before her.*]

EMPRESS

To the Daughter of the Mings, what message can
the Tartar Emperor have?

EMPEROR [*Seeing her hands bound with the silken cord*]

Oh! but your hands are tied! I ordered that to
save you from yourself. But now! [*He approaches, yet hesitates to touch her hands. The*
EMPRESS *draws back, gazing at him for the first
time.*] Oh! pardon —— Before you, in the depth
of my grief, I had forgotten. I had almost dared
to touch your bruised hands. And yet you are more
sacred to me here than there in Nanking, in all
your splendour. [*He strikes the gong softly. An*
OFFICIAL *appears.*]

EMPEROR [*To the* OFFICIAL]

Let the Governess of the Palace come here at once! [*To the* GOVERNESS, *as she enters and prostrates herself.*] Untie the hands of the Empress, and then go.

[*The* GOVERNESS *obeys and goes out. A pause.*]

Your voice is no longer yours. Your eyes are no longer yours. You stand here before me, yet your soul seems to be at an infinite distance. I did not expect to find you so, and you frighten me. The Majesty of death is upon you.

EMPRESS

They are calling to me from the Land of the Shades. Allow me to cross the threshold soon, from you I can accept no mercy. My faithful ones, my warriors, are wondering at my delay in rejoining them, and my son is listening to catch the echo of my footfall behind him on the dark path.

EMPEROR

Your son!—— Ah! Your son! Who has mourned him more than I, excepting only you? Ten of my couriers, my swiftest horsemen, were sent at once, riding their horses night and day, spurring them to death, leaving their corpses by the roadside, in a frantic effort to arrive in time and avert the evil which could not be repaired ——

EMPRESS

What was achieved?   Where is the body of my little son?

EMPEROR

It is now in an imperial hearse, making its slow way to the north, preceded by funeral music, followed by a thousand dignitaries in costumes of state befitting the rank of a young sovereign.

EMPRESS

And where are they taking him, my son?

EMPEROR

To those inviolable forests where the Tartar Emperors repose.   There, in a vale, which the spade of men has never touched, two leagues of dark cedars will envelope in their silence, his tomb built all of porcelain.

EMPRESS

Will you grant me the favour to sleep near him?

EMPEROR   [*Very gently, speaking like a child*]
But —— in accordance with the custom of the Empresses, you will yourself choose the site and scene in the forest and will have the long marble avenues built —— so that all may be in readiness when your hour strikes.

EMPRESS

My hour *has sounded* — ah! many days ago.
I heard it, but my hands were tied and your guards
were ever about me.   Now you will give me my last
freedom, will you not? so that I may join all the
dead heroes who are awaiting me.   To keep me
back would be unworthy of you, my noble enemy.
You would not do that! ——

EMPEROR   [*After a pause*]

Keep you back, you? ——   O! no, not I ——
But your duty —— Daughter of the Mings, you
are incapable of failing in your duty!

EMPRESS   [*Excitedly at last*]

My duty! What duty? Already have I been
decoyed by that word.   They urged me thereby to
flee like a common woman beset by fear.   While
all my brave defenders knew how to die heroically,
my soldiers, my princes, even my ladies-in-waiting, I like a coward escaped through the subterranean passages of my palace —— to fulfil my
duty!   It was the hour when my soldiers were falling by the thousand, struck down by yours, when my
walls were crumbling under the assault of your
armies —— the draught of the Great Deliverance
had been brought me in a cup, and I was calm as I
am now — but smiling.   I was about to raise the

cup to my lips, to pass beyond the reach of all, proud and inviolable, in my imperial attire. The vaults beneath the ground, the sleeping place of my ancestors, unknown to your Tartars, stood open close at hand, and there was still time to carry me down into them —— But duty! Ah! my duty, it appeared, was to flee, and I yielded —— And until the day when your soldiers took me captive, I wandered on and on through the country, at the head of my defeated troops —— I, the Empress, the Invisible, desecrating my majesty among all those thousands of men —— marching before them like some mad woman! ——

EMPEROR

Say rather that you were the sublime heroine, the great warrior-Empress, the goddess of battle, who braved arrows and bullets, and will live on eternally in poetry and history!

EMPRESS

I sought to justify my flight, that was all. I did all I could, but none can ever atone for a cowardly action. It was in my own palace that I should have met my death, in the funeral fire lighted by my own hand, in which so many heroes were consumed —— My ashes should have mixed with theirs. Duty, do you say? But do you believe that I still belong to Earth? My cities are in ruins, my armies annihilated, my son dead. And at this very moment I know that one by one the heads of my few remaining soldiers are falling into the dust beneath your high Tartar walls. Then what duty remains, I ask you? [*She takes the dagger from the fold of her robe and raises her hand to strike herself.*] Nothing, nothing but this! [*The* EM-PEROR *rushes towards her with a cry, seizes her wrist, takes the dagger, and hurls it to the ground.*] Ah! So you dare to touch me now?

EMPEROR [*Bowing very low*]

Your pardon! Only listen to me. You may die afterwards if you wish it, I promise you — but in some less terrible way —— without this bloodshed. I will even furnish you the means, if you still wish it ——

EMPRESS [*With sudden gentleness*]

In some less terrible way! Yes, that is what I desire. The Potion of the Great Deliverance, we sovereigns are never without it. You have it too, have you not?

EMPEROR

Night and day within easy reach, especially since you began to risk your life hourly, in the thick of the battle. I feared that I should be unable to cap-ture alive my beautiful Phœnix of War! Be

assured, we have the Deliverance. It is in this
golden case, among the trinkets at my girdle.

EMPRESS

And you will give it to me?

EMPEROR

Yes.

EMPRESS

You swear it?

EMPEROR

Yes. After you have listened to me, I shall have
this supreme courage. To refuse you would be unworthy of you and of myself. But, after you
have heard me, only afterwards ——

EMPRESS

Well, speak, sire. In return for your promise,
take the last minutes in which my ears can hear,
my eyes can see ——

SCENE VIII.

The same. An OFFICIAL

EMPEROR [*He strikes the gong gently, an* OF-
FICIAL *appears. To the* OFFICIAL] Double the
number of guards at the gates. Instant death to

any one who, for any reason whatever, dares to open that door before I sound the gong *Three Times!* Is that understood? You may go!

[*The* OFFICIAL *turns to go.*]

Wait! [*Pointing to the incense-burners on the steps of the throne.*] Incense! Let the sticks be lighted at once! I must have perfume in the air. [*The* OFFICIAL *hastily lights the bundles of sticks and the smoke rises.*] It is well, go!

[*The* OFFICIAL *makes his exit backward, almost prostrate.*]

SCENE IX.

The EMPEROR   [*To the* EMPRESS, *who is leaning against the balustrade of the throne*] Alas! I can read obstinate resolution in your eyes! You have determined to die, I know it! I shall speak without hope. Will you grant me one last favour?

EMPRESS

No doubt I shall. But what may it be?

EMPEROR   [*Pointing to the throne*]

Let our last interview take place there! Once in your life, though it be on a day which shall know no to-morrow, I wish to see you seated upon the throne of the Tartar conquerors.

EMPRESS [*Very calmly and indifferently*]

Is it only that? If that will give you pleasure, I consent. [*She begins to ascend the steps.*] I mount but slowly: I am crushed and fainting. The poison which you promised lulls one to sleep, does it not? It does not sharpen and distort the features, I hope. The Phœnix, even in the agony of death would wish to retain some charm.

EMPEROR [*In the same mood*]

It is even better than you hope. It comes from the Western Barbarians. Lustrous pearls under a thin leaf of gold. One passes into space in a sudden sleep, an exquisite intoxication ——

EMPRESS [*Still far away*]

Ah! —— in a sleep — [*They have reached the top of the steps. She half reclines across the throne, which is almost as large as a divan. The* EMPEROR *remains standing.*] Well, now —— delay no longer, speak ——

EMPEROR

It was not the prompting of a mere whim which urged me to see you seated there. What we have to say is so solemn. The interview of an Emperor and an Empress, power speaking to power! —— At this height, raised above our earthly personalities, we shall feel more conscious of our superhuman mission.

EMPRESS

Power speaking to power? I am no longer anything but a captive, who counts for naught.

EMPEROR

You are sovereign and doubly sovereign now, mistress of the destiny of China, arbiter of all. [*The* EMPRESS *looks at him as though deeply hurt.*] Mistress of the destiny of China, yes! Be not offended. I do not intend to speak of your power over the Emperor —— But, defeated and captive, what does it matter? Are you not always the Daughter of the Mings? Hundreds of millions of hearts bear secret allegiance to you. The rebellion quelled to-day by my soldiers will break out afresh to-morrow, will always be renewed. You are the only being in the world who has the power to still it for ever —— and that takes away the right to die ——

EMPRESS [*Interrupting*]

The dead await me —— I belong to them now —— I hear their voices calling to me to come ——

EMPEROR

I want to tell you in the fewest words. But I feel as though you were already gone, already cold.

I press on and I am all at a loss. It seems as if I were speaking to a tombstone. Powers, you and I, I said, ah, yes, great powers! Two rival lives of fabled emperors, of deified heroes, growing feebler and feebler by centuries of slavery to rites and forms, prisoners in an excess of luxury; two dynasties that seemed doomed to an immortality of mummyhood, have by some miracle produced you and me, who are alive and young. As a result of our union, a new China might arise, living like us, to dominate the world. Together we might accomplish that holy mission for the well-being and happiness of our races, and the eternal glory of our two united names. But without you, no, I can do nothing. I shall sink again into my gilded solitude, my sickly idleness, my opium-drugged sleep. If you but knew my youth, how isolated and lonely, spent in an apartment decorated in black ebony! In the gloom of this palace, an imaginative child, I outlined this glorious plan of union with you. It haunted my brain. Then your son would have been my son. It was like a child still that I set out on that adventure to see you in your palace at Nanking. And as I beheld, my man's will, which still floated in the midst of dreams, was suddenly concentrated upon one definite desire. Ah, what obstacles I overcame! First, I had to escape from your palace; then to return here unhindered within the terrible walls of the Yellow City; and then to wrest the power from those grim evil-doers who had so long tortured my youthful will and my reason. The war was already at its height, hatred was enchained, the smell of blood was in the air, and Chinese and Tartars were howling like wild beasts. All this, you know full well, I was unable to stop.

EMPRESS

I know.

EMPEROR

That I did all in my power to save your son — you believe that, do you not?

EMPRESS

Now I believe it.

EMPEROR

My only reason for speaking of these things is that at least you may not hate me.

EMPRESS [*Still calm and impersonal*]
I have no hate for you.

EMPEROR

The heads of your faitthful soldiers which have just fallen were sacrificed against my will. I had issued an order of unconditional pardon. As to the Prince who left you a few minutes ago. [*Smiling*] — for I see all, I the Phantom Emperor, as you called me — yes, he who was speaking to you in this very place and went so heroically to meet his death, will be saved.   You shall see him again!

EMPRESS

I thought you before now a great and generous enemy.

EMPEROR

Of my love I have not even dared to speak to you.

EMPRESS

I am grateful to you that you have kept our interview above that level.

EMPEROR

Every word you utter falls upon me like the icy drops of slow winter rain, and yet withal I must have the force to proceed to the end.   Listen to what I now shall say; it is the last word I shall speak, after that you will be free.   Despite that dreadful war to the death between us, despite that funeral procession which now slowly carries your son to the forests of the Last Repose, I still indulged in the beautiful dream of putting an end to ancient hates by means of our marriage, of making one our two rival dynasties, of giving to the great empire peace everlasting ——

EMPRESS   [*Interrupting*]

Ever since you asked me to be seated upon your throne, I understood.

EMPEROR   [*After a pause*]

And your reply?

EMPRESS

My reply is that, neither living nor dead, will I permit the Emperor of the Tartars even to touch my hand. It is too late; too many rivers of blood flow between us.

EMPEROR

Still one word, one last word. We are not alone at this solemn historical hour, in this place which seems so empty and silent. The shades of warriors and the illustrious spirits of departed emperors are all about us, listening anxiously for your decision. Your beloved dead are all here, at peace with mine in the lofty harmony of heaven. You are mistaken, they are not calling to you to join them; they are commanding you to live for years to come, to aid me in this great work of peace, of which I dream and which, without you seated at my side on this throne, I shall be powerless to carry out. You have not the right to decline this duty! In the name of the thousands of invisible spirits who surround us, I beg of you, Daughter of

Heaven, to live! [*A silence.*] I have said all that I find possible to say I await your decision. I have finished.

EMPRESS [*Growing colder and more distant in her attitude, pointing to the golden jewel-case attached to the* EMPEROR'S *girdle*] Then give it to me now!

EMPEROR [*In absolute despair*]

No, no! Give it to you with my own hands I cannot. Have pity —— I cannot! I cannot!

EMPRESS [*Severely*]

But your promise, sire, your imperial word of honour. Give it to me!

[*The* EMPEROR, *after another silence, kneels before her, takes the golden box from his girdle and hands it to her slowly, his face turned downward to the ground.*]

EMPRESS [*After opening the box, speaking gently, like a child in a dream.*] Yes, they are tiny, shining pearls —— And they will bring death, peace, nothingness. [*She puts the pearls in her mouth, then throws the box to the ground, and rises in exaltation. Triumphant and dominating the room, she addresses the invisible spirits of her forefathers.*] Oh, my ancestors, behold me! Am

I not glorious? You see me in that place whence you of old dominated the world, and it is upon your throne, usurped by the Tartar, that I am about to die! Your daughter has remained worthy of her race. Despite temptation more than human, she has kept her word. Open wide before the portals of death,— to receive her among you. [*Smiling and quite gentle, she turns to the* EMPEROR *who is still kneeling.*] And now that my mission is accomplished, approach me, sire. [*She takes his hand gently, to indicate that he may rise and be seated.*] For the second time in her life, the Empress invites you to be seated in her presence, as once before, over there, you remember, one morning in my palace which is now no more —— [*She seats herself on the throne again.*]

EMPEROR [*Dreamily*]

As once before, there in your garden on that never-to-be-forgotten morning. All about us, the wonderful flowers of distant lands were unfolding their petals, still moist with the early dews —— and the beautiful Imperial Phœnix was brilliant in all her glory. [*He seats himself on the throne near her, his head resting against the back.*]

EMPRESS

To-day, the flames have swept away those flowers, and the Phœnix is in agony, her wings burned in

the fire of war. But, on the threshold of
the Great Beyond, she will confide to you her deep-
est secret. Now it is your turn to listen. [*The*
EMPEROR *raises his head and looks at her.*] While
you were uttering those noble and magnificent
words of sacrifice —— Oh! beneath my impassive
mask, what a struggle was mine on to be deaf to
their appeal! And I should have yielded, if the
duty which you presented to me had been only a
painful duty. But it would have been too easy
and too sweet. For I loved you! [*The* EMPEROR
arises.] And, living, I have no more the right to
happiness, because it was I who lighted that great
funeral pyre of men's lives in my palace.

EMPEROR   [*Interrupting, exultantly*]

O my sovereign! O my beautiful, fading flower!
To hear that from your lips at the moment when
they are about to grow cold for ever! Oh! To be
beloved by you, I could not believe it possible.
And now no aid can come from men or gods.

EMPRESS

No aid? Do you think I would accept it? I
have spoken only because I know I am going to die.
Aid! But did I not tell you it was I who lighted
the pyre, this hand which set to it the flaming torch.
And as they threw themselves into the glowing fur-
nace, dying for my son and for me, I cried out my

solemn vow: Soon I come to the Land of the Shades, I come, I follow you. After that, if I were to live, to spend a happy life with you —— I should loathe myself. [*She remains seated, the* EMPEROR *kneels at her feet, resting his head on the cushions of the throne.*] In entering your palace, I was afraid of myself, it was only myself that I feared —— for at no time did I hate that strange impostor who appeared in my palace one day, never did I hate him even when I knew not, when I did not understand. And in the closed litter in which I was brought to Peking, at every stage of that mournful journey my fears and my anguish increased, according as the impression became stronger and stronger, until at last I was convinced that you were the Emperor! [*Suddenly terrified, she starts up.*] You have not deceived me? Tell me, it is indeed death which you have given me? Oh, no, you could not have done that. You are too noble to have led me into a trap——

EMPEROR

No, my sovereign, no, I have not deceived you. Death is close to you, it is in your heart, inevitable death.

EMPRESS

Will it take long? How many minutes are still left to me?

EMPEROR

Minutes? Oh, scarcely seconds. You are on the point of slipping away from me into nothingness. The frail covering of gold leaf still protects you. As soon as that dissolves ——

EMPRESS

I shall suffer?

EMPEROR

No!

EMPRESS

Tell me how I shall pass away.

EMPEROR

You will hear a ringing in your brain as if the great bell of honour were being sounded for you — and then a dizziness — and suddenly will come eternal peace! [*He rises and rends his garments.*] O Gods, if you are capable of compassion, look down upon me —— have pity!

EMPRESS [*At first very slowly, pacing the platform of the throne like one in a dream.*] Whither am I going? Who can tell me whither I am going, where I shall soon be? To the dead? to the Shades, what can it matter how I use this last flicker of my life, so soon to be extinguished? Now that I have kept my word, at least this last moment belongs to me, which to us is worth Eternity. [*To*

the EMPEROR.] Let it be mine that I may give it
to you! [*She seats herself on the throne again.*]
Come close to me, my beloved, my master, my God
—— [*The* EMPEROR *sits near her, at first as with
religious awe.*] Come, I desire to rest my head on
your shoulder while I die —— [*The* EMPEROR
takes her in his arms.] Do you not see that we are
like two stars, separated by a boundless abyss, but
withal making desperate efforts to flash their light
to each other? —— But now the abyss is crossed
and my mortal enemy is weeping tears for love in
my embrace. Let me rest against your breast, come
closer, with all your being, that I may pass away as
though in you.

EMPEROR [*Embracing her more passionately*]

In me and with me, for I shall follow you, my
beautiful Phœnix, that would fly away beyond my
reach ——

EMPRESS

No! Remain on earth, live on to keep the love
which I have given you. Who else would remember me and pay the honours to my spirit? In the
valley of eternal silence, amid the marble avenues,
under the shade of the dark cedars, who else would
come to dream of my vanished beauty, that was but
for a day? Promise me you will stay. But come
still closer to me. If you do not fear the last breath
of one who is dying, press your lips against mine,

my beloved, that I may at least have known the rapture of your kiss ——

EMPEROR [*Pressing his lips to hers desperately*]
Oh! Even your ashes would be lovely to me, even your body in decay. Fear! you ask if I fear? Respect alone will unlock my embrace — when I feel that the breath of life is no more.

EMPRESS [*Wandering, half drawing herself away*]
Ah! Yes — I hear the great bell sounding. It is the signal, then? I am sinking —— Hold me up, my beloved. Keep me from sinking thus —— into the abyss.

[*During an instant of silence, they remain embraced. Then the* EMPEROR *rouses himself, cries aloud in his grief, and the dead body falls back on the throne.*]

SCENE X.

The EMPEROR, *and then the* CROWD.
[*The* EMPEROR *descends the steps of the throne, quickly runs to the gong and strikes three deep strokes. The doors are thrown open.* DIGNITARIES *and* OFFICIALS *appear on the threshold.*]
The EMPEROR [*addressing the crowd, who enter*

in robes of state, and pointing to the dead Empress.]

Come, all dignitaries and great men of the Empire! Put perfumes in the censers, keep on amber! Sound the marble chimes, as for the gods. Pay homage to Your Empress! On your knees, all, before The Daughter of Heaven!——

[*He kneels on the steps himself The marble chimes are sounded. The brilliant crowd fills the throne-room, prostrating themselves before the dead.*]

THE END